Phonics, Phonemic Awareness, and Word Analysis for Teachers: An Interactive Tutorial

Tenth Edition

Donald J. Leu
University of Connecticut

Charles K. Kinzer
*Teachers College,
Columbia University*

PEARSON

Boston   Columbus   Indianapolis   New York   San Francisco
Amsterdam   Cape Town   Dubai   London   Madrid   Milan   Munich   Paris   Montréal
Toronto   Delhi   Mexico City   São Paulo   Sydney   Hong Kong   Seoul   Singapore   Taipei   Tokyo

Vice President and Editorial Director: Jeffery Johnston
Executive Editor: Meredith D. Fossel
Editorial Assistant: Maria Feliberty
Executive Marketing Managers: Christopher Barry and Krista Clark
Program Manager: Miryam Chandler
Project Manager: Karen Mason
Manufacturing Buyer: Deidra Skahill
Full-Service Project Management: Lumina Datamatics, Inc.
Rights and Permissions Research Project Manager: Tania Zamora
Manager, Cover Visual Research & Permissions: Diane Lorenzo
Cover Image Credits: MirMar/Fotolia
Printer/Binder: LSC Communications
Text Credits: Credits and acknowledgments borrowed from other sources and reproduced, with permission, in this textbook appear on appropriate page within text. pp. 21, 40, 52, 83, 116: Used by permission from National Council of Teachers of English; pp. 14, 22, 41, 53, 65, 73, 83, 96, 104, 116–117: A courtesy of Apple Inc.

Cataloging in Publication data is available upon request

23 2023

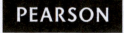

ISBN 10:   0-13-416978-6
ISBN 13: 978-0-13-416978-1

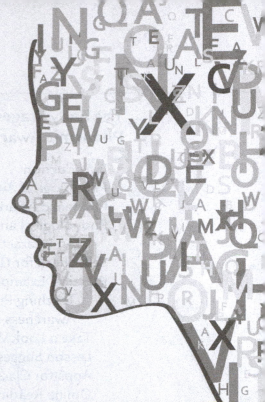

Contents

Preface	ix

1 Recognizing Words: Helping Children Develop Word Analysis Strategies

	1
Introduction	1
Phonological Awareness	2
Phonemic Awareness	2
Phonics	3
Context Use	3
Sight Word Knowledge	4
Morphemic Analysis	4
Chunking Words	4
Dictionary Skills	4
Developmental Spelling Patterns	5
Two Special Populations	5
English Learners	5
Struggling Readers	6
The Journey Ahead	6
Word Analysis: An Interactive Tutorial	6
Self-Check for Chapter 1	12
Practical Examples and Resources for Teaching Word Analysis in Your Classroom	13
Take a Look Videos	13
Lesson Suggestions	13
Apps for Classroom Use	13
Online Reading Resources	14

2 **The Early Stages: Phonological and Phonemic Awareness** **15**

    Introduction   15

    Phonological Awareness   15

    Phonemic Awareness   16

    Phonological and Phonemic Awareness:

        An Interactive Tutorial   17

    Self-Check for Chapter 2   20

    Practical Examples and Resources for

        Teaching Phonological and Phonemic

        Awareness in Your Classroom   21

        Take a Look Videos   21

        Lesson Suggestions   21

        Apps for Classroom Use   22

        Online Reading Resources   22

3 **Phonics: Onset, Rime, and Consonant Patterns** **23**

    Introduction   23

    Onset, Rime, and Consonant Patterns:

        An Interactive Tutorial   24

    Onset: Initial Consonants   24

    Rime   25

    Table 1. *The 37 Most Common Rime Patterns*   25

    Consonant Patterns   26

        Consonant Clusters   26

        Consonant Digraphs   27

        Consonant Blends   29

        Special Consonant Patterns   30

        Silent Consonant Patterns   35

    Self-Check for Chapter 3   38

    Practical Examples and Resources for

        Teaching Phonics (Onset, Rime, and

        Consonant Patterns) in Your Classroom   39

        Take a Look Videos   39

        Lesson Suggestions   40

        Apps for Classroom Use   40

        Online Reading Resources   41

4 Phonics: Vowel Patterns   43

Introduction	43
Vowel Patterns: An Interactive Tutorial	43
Single Vowels	44
Vowel Clusters	46
Vowel Digraphs	46
Vowel Blends (Diphthongs)	46
Vowel Generalizations	47
Vowel Generalization 1 (CVC or VC)	48
Vowel Generalization 2 (CV)	48
Vowel Generalization 3 (VCE)	49
Vowel Generalization 4 (VV)	49
Self-Check for Chapter 4	50
Practical Examples and Resources for Teaching Phonics (Vowel Patterns) in Your Classroom	51
Take a Look Videos	51
Lesson Suggestions	52
Apps for Classroom Use	52
Online Reading Resources	53

5 Context   55

Introduction	55
The Importance and Use of Context: An Interactive Tutorial	56
Using Context to Check Word Analysis	57
Using Context with Other Word Analysis Techniques	57
Using Context as a Basic Word Analysis Technique to Determine Meaning	59
Limitations of Using Context Clues	62
Self-Check for Chapter 5	63
Practical Examples and Resources for Teaching Context Skills in Your Classroom	64
Take a Look Videos	64
Lesson Suggestions	64
Apps for Classroom Use	65
Online Reading Resources	65

6 Sight Words   67

Introduction	67
The Devlopment of Sight Word Knowledge: An Interactive Tutorial	67
Figure 1 *Dolch List of Basic Sight Words*	69
Self-Check for Chapter 6	71

Practical Examples and Resources for Teaching
    Sight Words in Your Classroom 72
    Take a Look Videos 72
    Lesson Suggestions 72
    Apps for Classroom Use 72
    Online Reading Resources 73

Morphemic Analysis 75

Introduction 75
Morphemic Analysis: An Interactive Tutorial 76
    Understanding Affixes 76
      Adding Prefixes 76
      Prefix Generalization 76
      Adding Suffixes 77
      Suffix Generalization 1 78
      Suffix Generalization 2 79
      Suffix Generalization 3 80
      Suffix Generalization 4 81
Self-Check for Chapter 7 81
Practical Examples and Resources for Teaching
    Morphemic Analysis in Your Classroom 82
    Take a Look Videos 82
    Lesson Suggestions 83
    Apps for Classroom Use 83
    Online Reading Resources 84

Chunking Words into Smaller Units: Syllabication and Structural Analysis 85

Introduction 85
Syllabication and Structural Analysis:
    An Interactive Tutorial 85
    Syllabication 85
      Syllabication Generalization 1 86
      Syllabication Generalization 2 86
      Syllabication Generalization 3 (VC/CV) 87
      Syllabication Generalization 4 (V/CV or VC/V) 88
      Syllabication Generalization 5 (V/digraph V
        or V/blend V) 89
      Syllabication Generalization 6 (Compound
        Words) 90
      Syllabication Generalization 7 90
      Syllabication Generalization 8 (V/C + le) 90

Using Syllabication to Help with Pronunciation 91
    Pronunciation Generalization 1 92
    Pronunciation Generalization 2 92
    Pronunciation Generalization 3 93
    Pronunciation Generalization 4 93
    Pronunciation Generalization 5 93
    Pronunciation Generalization 6 94
Self-Check for Chapter 8 95
Practical Examples and Resources for Teaching
    Chunking Skills in Your Classroom 96
    Take a Look Videos 96
    Lesson Suggestions 96
    Apps for Classroom Use 96
    Online Reading Resources 97

The Dictionary and Word Analysis   99

Introduction 99
The Dictionary and Word Analysis: An Interactive
    Tutorial 99
    Locating Words in a Dictionary 99
    Using a Dictionary to Help Determine Pronunciation 100
    Using a Dictionary to Help Determine Meaning 101
Self-Check for Chapter 9 102
Practical Examples and Resources for Teaching
    Dictionary Skills in Your Classroom 103
    Take a Look Videos 103
    Lesson Suggestions 104
    Apps for Classroom Use 104
    Online Reading Resources 104

Developmental Spelling Patterns: Insights into the Development of Word Analysis Skills   105

Introduction 105
    Figure 1 *The Leu and Kinzer Developmental*
      Spelling Checklist 107
Developmental Spelling Patterns: An Interactive Tutorial 108
    The Precommunicative Phase 108
      Figure 2 *An Example of a Child's Writing from the*
      Precommunicative Phase 108
    The Semiphonetic Phase 109
      Figure 3 *An Example of a Child's Writing from the*
      Semiphonetic Phase. ("I Read the Book.") 109

The Phonetic Phase   110

    Figure 4 *An Example of a Child's Writing from*
    the Phonetic Phase. ("Frogs Jumped.")   111

The Transitional Phase   112

    Figure 5 *An Example of a Child's Writing*
    from the Transitional Phase   112

The Standard Phase   113

    Figure 6 *An Example of a Child's Writing*
    from the Standard Phase   113

Self-Check for Chapter 10   114

Practical Examples and Resources for
    Understanding Developmental Spelling
    Patterns in Your Classroom   116

Take a Look Videos   116

Lesson Suggestions   116

Apps for Classroom Use   116

Online Reading Resources   117

Posttest I   **119**

Posttest II   **125**

References   **131**

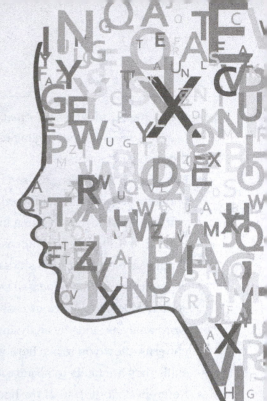

Preface

NEW TO THIS EDITION

This edition continues the evolution of this classic work that saves course time and maximizes students' control over their learning. Our self-paced tutorial approach allows readers to independently study and learn the important aspects of phonics, phonemic awareness, and word analysis, which saves time in class and prepares them for the state reading exams, now required in many states. The substantial amount of course time normally needed for teaching these topics can instead be devoted to other material, while ensuring that students fully understand these essential elements of reading instruction. Two posttests at the end of the book may be used to ensure that the content has been mastered.

In this tenth edition, we have made the following changes:

- Each chapter contains a substantially expanded section on instructional practice that will help teachers new to word analysis instruction begin their important work in this area. For teachers refreshing their knowledge, the sections relating to instructional practice provide suggestions that can be immediately used in their classrooms.
- Two new sections have been added to each chapter: "Take a Look Videos" and "Apps," which provide links to videos and apps that further explain or extend the chapter's content. Both will help in-service and preservice teachers compile important teaching resources and ideas.
- Each chapter includes an updated set of online reading resources. These resources will help readers extend their understanding of each chapter's topic.

- Each chapter includes information about how best to support English Learners as well as struggling readers so that we provide optimal support to these special populations.
- Each chapter has been revised to include the latest research on phonics, phonemic awareness, and word analysis. This will keep readers up-to-date with the most recent thinking in these areas.
- Each chapter has been condensed to focus on essential elements. This should save time for both students and course instructors.
- We conclude with an updated section that enables you to quickly diagnose students' developing awareness of their phonic, phonemic awareness, and word analysis skills by analyzing their writing. Developmental spelling patterns allow you to see both what students know and what word analysis skills they are likely to acquire next on their journey.
- References at the end of the book have been updated and include online sources.

Our purpose in this edition is to provide practical information about phonemic awareness, phonics, and word analysis for preservice teacher education and in-service teachers who are updating their knowledge or preparing for examinations. These areas continue to be important for beginning reading instruction.

Although we focus on phonics, phonemic awareness, and word analysis, it is important to be clear about the relationship between word analysis strategies and meaning construction. Meaning must be the focus of all reading, and word analysis should be viewed as one of many strategies necessary for constructing meaning from printed language. We believe that word analysis strategies are important in a balanced program of reading, especially in the early stages, but it is also important to keep in mind that readers bring meaning to their texts as they decode the meaning in printed materials.

We feel that teachers need information about a wide range of word analysis strategies: phonological and phonemic awareness, onset and rime patterns, phonic generalizations with high utility, context use, sight word knowledge, developmental spelling phases, morphemic and structural analysis, and using various dictionary resources. In learning to read, children must acquire effective strategies for recognizing unfamiliar words. Each child, however, is an individual. No single strategy will meet the needs of every child in a classroom. We believe that children learn best when they have an insightful teacher who is capable of making professional judgments about what each child requires. We also believe that the information in this text will help readers to develop the insights about word analysis that are so critical to children successfully starting their reading journeys.

Finally, while we have attempted to provide current and useful online resources, between the time website information is gathered and then published, some sites may have closed, some videos may no longer be available, and the cost of Apps may have changed. We would appreciate knowing about sites or resources that you are unable to access. Also, if you find or use sites that you believe to be particularly helpful and would like to share them, please send us a link for consideration as a resource to be included in the next edition.

ACKNOWLEDGMENTS

We would like to thank the reviewers of our manuscript for their insights and comments: Carolyn Abel, Stephen F. Austin State University; Jennifer P. Bailey, University of West Florida; Amy Barnhill, University of Houston-Victoria; Alice J. Feret, Ed. D., East Carolina University; Deborah Owens, Arkansas State University; Joan Powell, Writing Specialist, Whitley County Board of Education, Williamsburg, KY; Denise A. Dole Tallakson, University of Northern Iowa; and Carol B. Tanksley, University of West Florida.

We also thank the reviewers of the previous edition: Jennifer P. Bailey, University of West Florida; Carol J. Fuhler, Iowa State University; Diane C. Greene, Mississippi State University; Bruce Gutknecht, University of North Florida; Tommy L. Hansen, University of Nebraska at Kearney; Rosie Webb Joels, University of Central Florida; Stacey Leftwich, Rowan University; Priscilla Manarino-Leggett, Fayetteville State University; Amy S. Meekins, Salisbury University; Gregory P. Risner, University of North Alabama; Ann Russell, Southwestern Oklahoma State University; Gail G. Smith, Ashland University; Carol B. Tanksley, University of West Florida; Josh Thompson, The University of Texas at Arlington; and John T. Wolinski, Salisbury University.

USING THIS TEXT

Effective use of this book can best be accomplished by following these strategies:

1. Cover the answer portion of the page with a piece of cardboard or Please make certain this perforated mask, on the back cover page, will appear in this edition as it has in others.
2. After you have written your answer in the appropriate blank, slide the mask down to expose the correct answer.
3. Read each frame carefully. Easy frames lead to more advanced frames that provide deeper understanding of the material.

4. Complete the review sections in each chapter as though they were tests. When you miss an item, check for the related entry in the chapter.
5. Take the final Self-Check and review as needed.

We wish you the very best in providing young children with the most important gift anyone can receive: the gift of literacy.

Donald J. Leu
University of Connecticut

Charles K. Kinzer
Teachers College,
Columbia University

ABOUT THE AUTHORS

Donald J. Leu is a graduate of Michigan State, Harvard, and the University of California, Berkeley. He is the Neag Endowed Chair in Literacy and Technology at the University of Connecticut and holds a joint appointment in the Departments of Curriculum and Instruction and Educational Psychology. He has served as a member of the Board of Directors of the International Reading Association and as President of the Literacy Research Association. He is a member of the Reading Hall of Fame.

Charles K. (Chuck) Kinzer holds graduate degrees from the University of British Columbia and the University of California, Berkeley. He is a Professor of Education in the Communication, Media and Learning Technologies Design Program at Teachers College, Columbia University, where he also directs the Game Research Laboratory. He works to affect positive changes in the teaching and learning of literacy, teacher professional development, and the use of technology in education more broadly. He is a past member of the Board of Directors of the Literacy Research Association.

1

Recognizing Words: Helping Children Develop Word Analysis Strategies

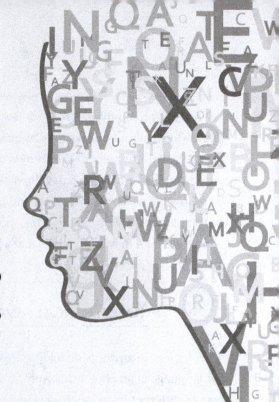

 ## INTRODUCTION

You are a proficient reader. When you read, you recognize most words without sounding them out. Most of the time, you recognize almost every word automatically, so you just think about the overall meaning of what you read. Your ability to recognize words rapidly and seemingly without effort is the foundation on which many other reading skills rest. How did you develop this ability?

Learning to read is a journey for every student. The paths of this journey are becoming increasingly clear to us, especially in the early stages when learning to recognize words is an important goal. We refer to children who are just beginning their literacy journeys as *emergent readers*.

Properly supported by their families and insightful teachers, emergent readers will develop effective word analysis strategies. These word analysis strategies lead to accurate and automatic word recognition and, ultimately, to effective reading comprehension.

Most printed words are unfamiliar to emergent readers. In the beginning, they do not even realize that printed words represent spoken words and they lack word analysis strategies to determine their oral equivalents. Emergent readers gradually develop these strategies, which are important to their development. Over time, most children develop the full range of word analysis strategies that enable them to become proficient readers, readers who are seldom conscious of these early skills that have become automatic.

What is word analysis? *Word analysis* refers to an extensive set of knowledge about our written language and strategies that permit readers to determine both the sounds of words and their meanings as they read. Word analysis develops as children acquire abilities in the following areas: phonological and phonemic awareness, phonics, context use, sight word knowledge, morphemic analysis, word "chunking," and dictionary skills. Let's look briefly at each area of word analysis.

PHONOLOGICAL AWARENESS

Phonological awareness develops when young children become aware that language is an object that may be analyzed and manipulated by them in different ways, such as rhyming, playing word games, and talking about words as objects. You can tell children have developed phonological awareness when they can hear words and syllables as separate units. We see evidence for phonological awareness when children are able to substitute one word for another at the end of a repeated sentence, play rhyming games in oral language, and segment a spoken word, such as the two syllables that make up the word *into*. An important beginning step on the way to phonemic awareness is becoming aware of language as an object that can be manipulated and analyzed.

PHONEMIC AWARENESS

Phonemes are the smallest unit of speech sounds, such as the three separate sounds you hear in the word *bead*. Phonemic awareness is being able to hear each sound as an individual unit.

What is the difference between phonological awareness and phonemic awareness? Put simply, when you possess phonological awareness, you are aware of individual words and syllables as objects. When you possess phonemic awareness, you are aware of individual sounds or phonemes as objects. With phonological awareness, you can hear and identify the two syllables in the spoken word *into*. With phonemic awareness, you can hear these two syllables and also hear and identify the two separate phonemes in the syllable *in* as well as the two phonemes in *to*.

Having phonemic awareness allows you to succeed in developing an awareness of the alphabetic principle, the next step on this journey. What is the alphabetic principle? It is the simple understanding that letters in our written language often represent sounds in a reasonably consistent manner. With an awareness of the alphabetic principle, having phonemic awareness enables you to develop specific aspects of phonic knowledge because you can identify the individual sounds in written words. If you cannot hear these sounds, phonics will provide little help. You can see that developing an awareness of phonemic knowledge is an important milestone in the development of word analysis.

PHONICS

Phonics, or sometimes called graphophonic knowledge, consists of several elements: (1) understanding the alphabetic principle, that is, letters in our written language often represent sounds in a reasonably consistent manner; (2) understanding the relationships between specific letters and the sounds that they often represent including common patterns that appear together; and (3) being able to put together, or blend, sounds represented by letters. Knowing the more regular letter–sound, or graphophonic, relationships helps us to recognize many words by permitting us to sound them out.

CONTEXT USE

Using context provides important assistance during word analysis. We can often anticipate what a word is, even before we actually have to read it by using the context that precedes the word. You use context, for example, when you read this sentence, recognizing the final word even though you do not see it: José opened the book and turned the _____. At other times, we can figure out an unfamiliar word by looking at the words and sentences that follow it. These examples represent *context use*, which is an important type of word analysis skill.

SIGHT WORD KNOWLEDGE

After we see a word many times, it eventually becomes a *sight word*, a word that we recognize instantly without having to analyze it with phonics or context use. High-frequency words, such as *me, I, you,* children's names, and others, quickly become sight words for us. As children become better readers, the words they know by sight, without the need to consciously analyze them, increases substantially. We seek to expand children's sight word knowledge because knowing just 200 of the most common words by sight will enable children to recognize about 50 percent of all the words they will encounter while reading.

MORPHEMIC ANALYSIS

Morphemic analysis refers to using prefixes and suffixes to break a word apart for both its meaning and pronunciation. Morphemic analysis is helpful in the later stages of word analysis in determining multisyllabic word meaning. Think about how you read words like *unachievable, plenipotentiary,* or *autobiographical.* You probably relied upon your morphemic analysis skills for both meaning and pronunciation.

CHUNKING WORDS

Chunking refers to breaking words into smaller units; it is sometimes called structural analysis or syllabication. Chunking can help determine a word's pronunciation and meaning. In this chapter, we include only those chunking or syllabication generalizations that are most useful and consistent.

DICTIONARY SKILLS

We sometimes use either an online or offline *dictionary* when analyzing the pronunciation or the meaning of a word. The skills used to both locate words and use entries to help us understand a word's pronunciation and meaning are sometimes important.

DEVELOPMENTAL SPELLING PATTERNS

Did you know that we can use an emergent reader's writing to determine what the child knows about reading, especially word analysis? The spelling patterns we see children use provide a window into their growing ability to recognize words. Uncorrected spelling patterns are especially revealing. A child who writes I LV MI CT ("I love my cat") tells us that he or she has both phonological and some phonemic awareness, understands the alphabetic principle, and knows much about graphophonic knowledge, or phonics, with initial and final consonants. This child, though, is only beginning to develop an awareness of vowels appearing in the middle of words.

If you know what to look for, children's developmental spelling patterns reveal important diagnostic information. They tell you what a child knows and does not know or at what stage a child is on the journey to becoming a fluent and automatic reader.

TWO SPECIAL POPULATIONS

While each child is unique and will require special instructional responses to support their word analysis development, there are two special populations to keep in mind as we explore this book: English Learners and struggling readers. Each helps us to understand the development of word analysis skills in richer and more powerful ways. English Learners accomplish word analysis in two written languages, not one—an exceptional accomplishment. It is also one where sometimes the patterns from the first language can help the student. At other times, the patterns from the first language make it more challenging. Struggling readers help us to understand the challenges of word analysis in especially profound ways. Their journeys are ones to admire and to inform us, helping each of us to become better literacy educators as we seek especially effective, and sometimes special, instructional practices to support their development. We will explore both populations in each chapter.

English Learners

English Learners acquire word analysis skills in English more easily when phonological and phonemic awareness are established in their first language before working to develop these in English. This, of course, is not always possible in school classrooms. We also know that phonics is more easily acquired when contextual support is provided and when analogic approaches are used to teach letter–sound relationships. Challenges also come from sound systems that are not always the same between the two languages. The general strategies suggested in this book may be modified appropriately and used to support these students, keeping in mind these specific areas of need.

Struggling Readers

Struggling readers take longer to develop reading skills that lead to accurate and automatic word recognition and, ultimately, to effective reading comprehension. These students often require additional instructional support, encouragement, and time. We want to pay particular attention to instructional practices and reading contexts that appear to yield the best results with struggling readers and maximize these practices and contexts in our work. We also need to provide particular encouragement, helping to sustain important motivation for reading. Finally, as with all students, we need to work closely with families, ensuring a positive supportive context at home for reading.

THE JOURNEY AHEAD

We will explore all of the elements of word analysis in this book for each of your students. Knowing about word analysis will help children as they begin to develop proficiency in reading. You will acquire an understanding about what young children must learn in the beginning stages of their journey. This will influence your decisions about what to teach young children to help them become successful readers.

WORD ANALYSIS: AN INTERACTIVE TUTORIAL

1. One element of reading instruction that teachers should be familiar with is word _____. Readers use word analysis to analyze written words and construct both their sounds and their _____.

analysis

meanings

2. Printed letters, words, and sentences are language symbols from which a reader seeks to derive _____. Word analysis refers to those strategies a reader uses when unfamiliar words are encountered in written _____. Both sound and meaning are _____ by the symbols in our written language.	meaning language represented
3. Readers construct meaning from written language. Although emergent readers are already familiar with the spoken form of their language, most of them are unfamiliar with the _____ form of language.	written
4. Many word _____ strategies are referred to as decoding skills. A reader must be able to use the knowledge of the _____ language code to decode words.	analysis written
5. *Phonics*, or *graphophonics*, is only one of many important word _____ strategies. Some elements of word analysis, such as phonological awareness and phonemic awareness, are skills that develop earlier. These enable readers to use word analysis _____.	analysis strategies
6. In reconstructing a message from written _____, a reader uses at least three types of cueing systems. These interrelated cueing systems are *graphophonics*, *semantics*, and *syntax*.	language
7. Grapho _____ information describes the relationship between sounds and the letters or spelling patterns making up written _____.	phonic language
8. Semantic information refers to the meaning elements of language. The vocabulary and conceptual background of a reader influence his or her ability to use _____ information.	semantic
9. Syntax refers to the sentence patterns and structure, or grammar, of _____. Readers use these structures, or _____ cues, when constructing meaning from print.	language syntactic

10. Readers use all three types of cueing systems, *graphophonics*, *semantics*, and *syntax*, simultaneously during the reading _____.	process
11. *Phonics* refers to the application of information about the sounds of _____ to the teaching of reading. The term *phonics* refers to the knowledge about how _____ are represented by letters or letter combinations in written language to help readers determine the oral equivalents of words. The English language does not have a completely predictable correspondence between sounds and written symbols, which makes phonics an incomplete word analysis system. Nevertheless, relationships between letters and sounds are sufficiently predictable to make _____ a useful word analysis strategy when it is combined with other strategies.	language sounds phonics
12. *Orthography* is the term used to refer to the writing system of a language. The writing system, or _____, of English is complex. English _____ is based on an alphabetic principle as well as morphological (word form) and syntactic considerations. Because of these additional influences, words are not always spelled the way they sound.	orthography orthography
13. A *phoneme* is the smallest single unit of sound in a language that distinguishes one *morpheme* (meaning unit) from another. For example, when the words *bit* and *sit* are spoken, only the first phoneme (out of three) is different. The spoken word *at* has two _____, whereas the spoken word *cat* has _____.	phonemes, three
14. A *grapheme* is a written or printed representation of a phoneme. For example, the letters <u>th</u>, <u>i</u>, and <u>s</u> in the word *this* each represent a grapheme. Note that a single grapheme may include several letters that represent a single sound such as <u>th</u>. When you see the written word *at*, you see two graphemes: _____ and _____. In the written word *path*, you see three _____: <u>p</u>, <u>a</u>, and <u>th</u>.	a t graphemes

15. The written word *chat* has four letters. It also has _____ graphemes and _____ phonemes. Two of the letters appear in a single grapheme, <u>ch</u>. This grapheme represents _____ sound.	three three one
16. In reading, children are expected to learn letter–sound relationships or, as they are frequently referred to, grapheme–phoneme _____.	relationships
17. Before they learn grapheme–phoneme relationships, however, most children become aware of words and syllabic units as discrete units. This is often referred to as _____ awareness.	phonological
18. _____ awareness is the general term used to label the conscious awareness about the sounds of language. Phonological _____ is an important milestone for young children because it indicates that they are consciously aware of the sounds of language and can analyze and manipulate these sounds in different ways.	Phonological awareness
19. If children can identify individual words in oral language, clap the syllables in a word, or know how to rhyme one word with another, we can be confident that they have developed _____ awareness.	phonological
20. A special aspect of phonological awareness, and a more challenging milestone, is the development of phonemic awareness. _____ awareness is demonstrated when a child can analyze and manipulate individual phonemes, or sounds, in oral language. Being able to identify all the sounds, or phonemes, in a spoken word, such as the two sounds in *at*, demonstrates that a child has phonemic _____.	Phonemic awareness
21. Phonemic awareness is important for children to develop because it enables them to benefit from _____ instruction.	phonics

22. Being able to determine the graphophonemic relationships in a word does not, by itself, always enable a reader to comprehend what he or she _____. However, graphophonemic cues can be combined with other language information to result in understanding what you read, or reading _____.	reads comprehension
23. A morpheme is the smallest unit of meaning in a language. The word *bookmark* has _____ morphemes.	two
24. Morphemic analysis refers to the analysis of words by using the meaningful parts of _____, such as prefixes, suffixes, contractions, compound words, and base words. Some use the term *structural analysis*; this term is equivalent to *morphemic analysis*. In addition, structural _____ includes the study of syllabic units in words and spelling patterns influenced by the addition of affixes.	words analysis
25. Morphemic _____ is concerned with how meaning is determined by the combination of morphemes, the smallest units of meaning in a language.	analysis
26. The word *box* contains one unit of meaning, or morpheme. In the word *boxes*, there are _____ morphemes: *box* and *es*. *Box* is called a free _____ because it can stand alone; another unit does not need to be added to it for the unit to have meaning. The *es* plural is an example of a bound morpheme. Bound morphemes function only when combined with a _____ morpheme.	two morpheme free
27. Morphemic analysis is an important aspect of word analysis. The use of morphemic analysis is limited, however, to words that contain identifiable morphemes, including _____, _____, and root words.	prefixes suffixes

28. The English spelling system is based on more than the correspondence between _____ and sounds. For example, consider the following word pairs: *sane* and *sanity*, *nation* and *national*, *democracy* and *democratic*. The sounds represented by the <u>a</u> in *sane* and *sanity*, the <u>a</u> in *nation* and *national*, and the <u>o</u> in *democracy* and *democratic* are not the same, even though these word pairs contain a basic meaning unit, or _____. Linguists use the term *morphophonemic* to refer to the combined meaning and _____ base of the English spelling system.	letters morpheme sound
29. Readers often use context clues during _____ analysis. Context clues require readers to rely on the other words and sentence patterning, or _____, in a reading selection, along with meaning cues in the material.	word syntax
30. _____ clues provide helpful information for determining word _____. Context clues are also helpful in determining pronunciation for readers who have previously heard a word orally but have never seen the printed form.	Context meaning
31. Efficient readers combine all _____ _____ techniques to figure out the pronunciation and _____ of unfamiliar words.	word, analysis meaning
32. Struggling readers take _____ to develop reading skills that lead to accurate and automatic word recognition and, ultimately, to effective reading comprehension.	longer
33. The ultimate aim of instruction in word analysis is to help students become more efficient readers. Efficient readers focus on meaning and recognize many words instantly. The words that readers _____ instantly comprise their sight _____ knowledge. One factor contributing to the development of extensive _____ word knowledge is a command of word analysis _____. Extensive _____ word knowledge also contributes to efficient reading.	recognize word sight strategies sight

34. English Learners acquire word analysis skills in English more easily when _____ and phonemic awareness are established in their first language.	phonological
35. Phonological awareness, phonemic awareness, phonics, context clues, sight words, structural and morphemic analyses, and using the dictionary are word _____ strategies discussed in this text. For children, this knowledge is acquired over a period of years. For you, this information is condensed into a brief, interactive tutorial to save you time.	analysis

☑ SELF-CHECK FOR CHAPTER 1

1. Readers use word _____ strategies to analyze written words in order to construct both sounds and meanings. Word analysis includes phonological and phonemic awareness, phonics, context use, sight word knowledge, morphemic analysis, and dictionary skills.	analysis
2. The term *graphophonic relationships* refers to the relationships between letters and _____.	sounds
3. The term *phonics* refers to how sounds are represented by _____.	letters
4. A _____ is the smallest single unit of sound in a language that distinguishes one morpheme from another.	phoneme
5. A _____ is a written or printed representation of a phoneme.	grapheme
6. The spoken word *push* has _____ phonemes.	three
7. The written word *past* has _____ graphemes.	four
8. When children are able to identify individual words and syllables in a language, we can be confident that they have developed _____ awareness.	phonological

9. When children are able to identify individual sounds, or phonemes, in a language, we can be confident that they have developed _____ awareness.	phonemic
10. A _____ is the smallest unit of meaning in a language. The word *running* has two morphemes.	morpheme
11. Readers often use surrounding words and other information, or _____ clues, during word analysis.	context
12. The words readers recognize instantly comprise their _____ word knowledge. Extensive sight word knowledge is important for efficient reading.	sight

PRACTICAL EXAMPLES AND RESOURCES FOR TEACHING WORD ANALYSIS IN YOUR CLASSROOM

Take a Look Videos

Take a look at this video of a teacher from New Zealand, teaching initial letter–sound correspondences to five-year-olds: http://bit.ly/1BMRPKx. This video illustrates a number of group instructional strategies for word analysis.

Lesson Suggestions

Starfall (http://www.starfall.com/). Use the online word analysis lessons from Starfall in your classroom. This valuable online resource contains activities within each of the areas discussed in this chapter and is designed for online use by children. The well-designed activities do not require users to provide identifying information about themselves or pay a fee to use the materials. It is the best-designed online experience for students in word analysis and early reading that we have encountered.

Apps for Classroom Use

Starfall Free: http://bit.ly/1AZ32Yo
Current cost: Free
This includes the Starfall Learn to Read section and the Short Vowel Pal books in an app format for iPads.

Looney Tunes Phonics: http://bit.ly/1siPzJa

    Current cost: Free

        For kindergarten through grade three, this app includes 100 lessons that teach phonic skills.

iSort Words: http://bit.ly/1xVzF8x

    Current cost: $1.99

        A game for students of age group 6–8 that helps them with letter patterns.

Short Vowel Word Study: http://bit.ly/1BN2Kns

    Current cost: $2.99

        Teaches short vowel sounds in an engaging fashion.

 ## Online Reading Resources

To learn more about word recognition and the important role it plays during the reading process, explore these online resources:

- Owens, K. (2009). Phonics on the web. An online tutorial exploring many aspects of phonics.

  Retrieved from http://www.phonicsontheweb.com/index.php

- Cunningham, P. M., & Cunningham, J. W. (2000). What we know about how to teach phonics. In S. E. Farstrup, S. J. Samuels (Eds.), *What research has to say about reading instruction* (pp. 87–109). Newark, DE: International Reading Association. (One of the best summaries of word recognition and phonics.)

  Retrieved from: http://www.learner.org/workshops/readingk2/support/HowToTeachPhonics_1.pdf

  http://www.learner.org/workshops/readingk2/support/HowToTeachPhonics_2.pdf

  http://www.learner.org/workshops/readingk2/support/HowToTeachPhonics_3.pdf

- Chard, D. J., & Dickson, S. V. (1999). Phonological awareness instructional and assessment guidelines. *Intervention in School and Clinic, 34*(5), 261–270.

  Retrieved from http://www.ldonline.org/article/6254

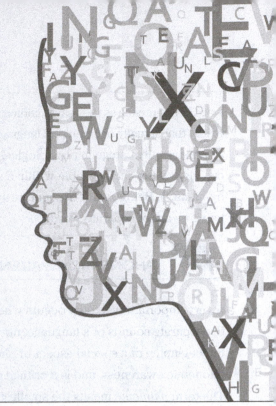

2

The Early Stages: Phonological and Phonemic Awareness

INTRODUCTION

Phonological awareness is a critical accomplishment for emergent readers. Phonological awareness exists when children become consciously aware that language is an object that may be analyzed and manipulated by them in different ways, such as rhyming, playing word games, and talking about words as objects.

PHONOLOGICAL AWARENESS

When young children first develop oral language, they use language to communicate and accomplish many goals that are important to them. Usually, however, they are not consciously aware of language as an abstract object that can be manipulated by them and others, taken apart and put back together in different ways, and analyzed. Initially, this might first happen when very young children play the "I wanna game" with an adult. An adult initiates this word game by saying, "I wanna *banana*," attempting to get the child to imitate the sentence while substituting a different noun at the end ("I wanna *apple/Snuffleupagus*/etc.") as each tries to use a sillier and sillier word until both of them end up laughing. Being able to manipulate language like this, substituting a number of different words in the same slot without any intent other than to play with language, is an example of phonological awareness. Another example of phonological awareness takes place when children can clap or tap each word in a sentence as they say it, indicating their awareness of individual words that actually occur in oral language as a continuous stream of sound.

A subsequent stage in phonological awareness exists when a child can clap or tap each syllable within a sentence or a word ("I want a ba-na-na."). Being aware of separate syllables is typically harder than being aware of separate words.

 ## PHONEMIC AWARENESS

A very important next step occurs when young children begin to hear the separate sounds of a language, not just words or syllables. This is the beginning of a special aspect of phonological awareness, called phonemic awareness, and is a critical stage in a child's literacy journey. The term *phoneme* means the smallest unit of speech sound. Phonemic awareness occurs when children become aware of individual phonemes in our language and can manipulate them in different ways. Phonemic awareness skills include sound matching, sound blending, sound isolation, sound addition, sound substitution, and sound subtraction.

We see evidence of this important milestone when children develop the ability to rhyme one word with another (*cat–pat*). Being able to play a rhyming game indicates phonemic awareness because a child is manipulating individual phonemes at the beginning of words. We also see evidence when a child can tell you the first sound at the beginning of a word, isolating it from others. Phonemic awareness also includes the ability to put several sounds together to form a single word. When you give a child several sounds (/k/–/at/) and he or she can blend them together to form an oral word (*cat*), we know that the child is developing phonemic awareness. This skill is essential for developing word analysis knowledge that is useful to read written language, such as phonic knowledge.

We use the term *phonological analysis* to refer to the conscious awareness of oral language as an object at the *word* and *syllable* level. We use the term *phonemic analysis* to refer to the conscious awareness of oral language as an object at the individual *phoneme* level. Phonological awareness is important because it gets the word analysis ball rolling as children begin to look at our language in an analytical manner. Phonemic awareness is important because it means that children are capable of analyzing the individual *sounds* of our language. This is essential to the successful development of phonic knowledge, which is an important aspect of word analysis.

Both phonological awareness and phonemic awareness can be taught and are important components of an early reading program. Many different instructional practices may be used to develop each element. Accommodations are typically made for English Learners and struggling readers. For English Learners, it is considered best if phonological and phonemic awareness are developed in the first language, initially. This makes it easier to develop these elements in English. Care needs to be paid to providing especially rich contests to develop phonological and phonemic awareness for English Learners.

Struggling, emergent readers often take longer to develop phonological and phonemic awareness. Care needs to be paid to ensure positive experiences so that they maintain motivation for reading and learning to read.

 ## PHONOLOGICAL AND PHONEMIC AWARENESS: AN INTERACTIVE TUTORIAL

1. Two aspects of oral language development that are important for developing word analysis skills and reading are _____ awareness and _____ awareness.	phonological phonemic
2. The definitions of phonological awareness and phonemic awareness differ among educators. Nevertheless, a common element in all definitions is that children who possess these abilities are consciously aware of language as an _____ that can be manipulated by them and others and analyzed.	object
3. In this book, we refer to _____ awareness as the conscious awareness of language as an object at the word and syllable level.	phonological
4. We refer to _____ awareness as the conscious awareness of language as an object at the individual sound, or phonemic, level.	phonemic
5. In oral language, being able to break up a word such as *dog* into the separate sound elements /d/, /o/, and /g/ demonstrates a high level of _____ awareness.	phonemic

6. Being able to break up a sentence into its constituent words demonstrates _____ awareness.	phonological
7. Being able to clap or tap each syllable in a word such as *table* demonstrates _____ awareness.	phonological
8. When a child is able to blend together the oral elements of a word such as *book*, we can say the child has developed an important aspect of _____ awareness.	phonemic
9. Usually, _____ awareness develops before _____ awareness.	phonological phonemic
10. The relationship between phonological/phonemic awareness and reading/writing is not unidirectional. Many children develop or enhance their phonological/phonemic awareness from their _____ experiences. They become more aware of language units—words and phonemes—from their interactions with print.	reading/writing
11. How do phonological and phonemic awareness work to help children become better readers and writers? First, being able to analyze oral language is likely to make it easier for children to think analytically about _____ language.	written
12. Second, analyzing the separate sounds in our language when phonemic awareness is achieved is likely to make it easier for children to match letters with _____, the content of phonics.	sounds
13. Third, phonemic awareness supports children in developing an awareness of the alphabetic principle; that is, letters in our written language often represent _____ in a reasonably consistent manner.	sounds
14. Did you know that phonemic awareness in kindergarten appears to be an excellent predictor of successful reading acquisition? This means that the extent to which children acquire _____ awareness in kindergarten predicts reasonably well their ability to learn to read in later grades.	phonemic

15. Although this is a powerful finding, it is not yet clear to what extent phonemic awareness causes success in reading or to what extent success in reading causes high levels of phonemic awareness. It is clear that learning to _____ will likely assist the development of phonemic awareness.	read
16. Phonemic awareness is not phonics, even though it makes the development of phonic knowledge easier. Phonics takes place in written language. Phonemic awareness takes place in _____ language.	oral
17. Most children, about 80 percent, develop _____ awareness by the middle of the first grade.	phonemic
18. The remaining 20 percent of children often find it challenging to learn to _____.	read
19. Often, these students become _____ readers and may require additional support with learning to read.	struggling
20. A logical outcome of this analysis of phonological awareness and phonemic awareness is that play with oral _____ should be included in a broad program of early literacy development for young children in preschool and kindergarten. These games would include nursery rhymes, word and sound riddles, songs, and poems. Teachers also use read-aloud books that manipulate the sounds of spoken language.	language
21. Oral language games and activities like these are important for all children but especially important for _____ Learners.	English
22. Phonemic awareness is not a single developmental milestone. Instead, it is a gradual process of an increasing ability to manipulate the _____ of language in different ways.	sounds
23. Rhyming ability, for example, appears much _____ than the ability to separate out each sound in a word such as *dog*.	earlier
24. One of the later abilities to develop is the ability to blend together separate _____ to construct a word such as *cat*.	phonemes

25. It is clear that phonemic awareness contributes in important ways to the development of early _____ skills.	reading

1. The conscious awareness of language as an object at the individual sound, or phonemic, level is important to later reading success. We refer to this as _____ awareness.	phonemic
2. Being able to identify individual words and syllables in spoken language is referred to as _____ awareness.	phonological
3. _____ awareness usually develops before _____ awareness.	Phonological, phonemic
4. A close relationship between the letters and sounds in a language is referred to as the _____ principle.	alphabetic
5. In kindergarten, an excellent predictor of later reading success is a child's level of _____ awareness.	phonemic
6. Young children who have a hard time developing phonemic awareness sometimes become _____ readers.	struggling
7. Phonemic awareness will likely assist in the development of _____, but the development of reading is also likely to extend a child's _____ awareness.	reading phonemic
8. About _____ percent of children develop phonemic awareness by the middle of the first grade.	80
9. Being able to tap the syllables in a word is an example of _____ awareness.	phonological
10. Achieving phonemic awareness is likely to make it _____ for children to learn phonics.	easier

PRACTICAL EXAMPLES AND RESOURCES FOR TEACHING PHONOLOGICAL AND PHONEMIC AWARENESS IN YOUR CLASSROOM

Take a Look Videos

Take a look at this video that shows a New Zealand teacher playing the game, "Syllable Sound Breaks" with five-year-olds: http://bit.ly/1yR1Ert. This teaches an important aspect of phonological awareness.

Take a look at this video that shows a teacher building phonemic awareness through "Silly Sound Attendance": http://bit.ly/1xPUxgV. This video shows a wonderful way to help students develop this important skill.

Lesson Suggestions

Building Phonemic Awareness with Phoneme Isolation (http://bit.ly/17uS9m5). This lesson contains games for kindergarten and first graders to identify whether a given sound occurs at the beginning or ending of a word.

Generating Rhymes: Developing Phonemic Awareness (http://bit.ly/1xPYjHb). This lesson from *ReadWriteThink* uses simple rhymes to build awareness of sound patterns. It helps young children become familiar with 12 rhyming pairs of one-syllable words. It gives them rhyming words for a given keyword in a poem and has them work with their peers to find additional rhyming pairs of word cards. It is especially useful for English Learners when matched with other students.

Phonemic Awareness and the Teaching of Reading. International Literacy Association. (1998). Newark, DE: International Literacy Association. A position statement from the Board of Directors of the International Literacy Association. This position statement (under revision) includes suggestions for the teaching of phonemic awareness, written by outstanding researchers and professionals in the field. Check frequently at www.literacyworldwide.org/ for updated position statements and teaching suggestions.

Apps for Classroom Use

Sound Beginnings: http://bit.ly/1vnzCPE

> Current cost: Free
>
>> This builds awareness of initial, ending, and medial sounds through a series of games.

ABC Matching Words Lite: http://bit.ly/1ACdHXJ

> Current cost: Free
>
>> A word rhyming and matching game.

Hearbuilder Phonological Awareness: http://bit.ly/1C1m3I9

> Current cost: Free
>
>> Students develop phonological awareness skills in a game as they earn instruments and band members to form a rock band while listening and learning to segment sounds and syllables.

Reading Raven: http://bit.ly/1tWjYxS

> Current Cost: $3.99
>
>> A very complete set of adventures designed to build early reading skills, including phonological and phonemic awareness.

Online Reading Resources

To learn more about phonological and phonemic awareness, explore these online resources:

- WETA. (2010). *Phonological and phonemic awareness*. Reading Rockets, Washington, DC: WETA (Explains both phonological and phonemic awareness and how children, teachers, and parents might see these in reading contexts).

  Retrieved from http://bit.ly/1y1xx0F

- Brummitt-Yale, J. (2010). *Phonemic awareness vs. phonological awareness*. (K-12 Reader. A short summary of the differences between phonemic awareness and phonological awareness.)

  Retrieved from http://bit.ly/1BNvWuC

3

Phonics: Onset, Rime, and Consonant Patterns

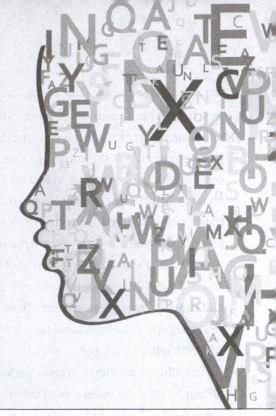

 INTRODUCTION

Phonics instruction involves teaching students two elements: (1) the relationship between letters and sounds and (2) how to blend sounds represented by letters. Sometimes this type of knowledge is referred to as graphophonic knowledge.

Letter–sound relationships in English are somewhat predictable and rule governed. The fact that many letters in English map reasonably well onto sounds is referred to as the *alphabetic principle*. The alphabetic principle is important for readers to come to recognize. In some languages, such as Spanish, the alphabetic principle applies nearly perfectly to the written language. In others, such as English, it applies with reasonable consistency, such that it provides a useful basis for word analysis. If English Learners are literate in a first language such as Spanish, the limited inconsistencies in letter–sound relationships in English may be areas that are challenging for them.

Understanding the specific patterns that relate letters to sounds is referred to as phonics, phonic knowledge, or graphophonic knowledge. Phonic knowledge and phonic/graphophonic strategies are important for successful word analysis. Being able to determine the oral equivalent of a written word often helps children determine a word's meaning.

Initial phonics instruction typically begins by teaching children common onset and rime patterns. Onset patterns include initial consonants found at the beginning of syllables and words, such as b̲, c̲, f̲. Rime patterns include a limited set of the most common endings to syllables and words, such as -at, -all, and others. By combining onset and rime patterns, children can quickly begin to apply the alphabetic principle to unlock the sounds of many written words; for example, *bat, cat, fat, ball, call, fall*, and so on. Onset and rime patterns are often an early component of phonics instruction. It is easier for children to use onset and rime patterns because they need to sound out and blend only two elements, not the many elements that might be required if they had to sound out long strings of letters in a word such as *importantly*. Struggling readers may especially benefit from an onset and rime approach, rather than learning all of the separate letter–sound relationships in isolation and then learning how to blend the sounds of separate letters together.

As children develop a greater understanding of the alphabetic principle, they are often taught other elements, including additional consonant patterns and vowel patterns. This chapter will cover onset and rime patterns as well as several additional consonant patterns, including consonant clusters, special consonant patterns, and silent consonant patterns. The next chapter will cover vowel patterns.

 ONSET, RIME, AND CONSONANT PATTERNS: AN INTERACTIVE TUTORIAL

 Onset: Initial Consonants

1. In English, single consonants contain the most consistent relationship between letters and _____.	sounds
2. Thus, instruction in the onset patterns of initial consonants, combined with preparation in common rime patterns, are almost always included during _____ instruction.	phonics
3. Some say that consonants also carry more information about words than _____, as seen in the following examples. The first sentence is missing every consonant. The second sentence is missing every vowel. Try to complete the missing letters in each sentence below. Which sentence is easier to complete? (a) _ _ e _ _ _ o _ e _ i _ e o _ _ o _ _ o _ a _ _ _! (b) S p _ n d m _ r _ t _ m _ _ n c _ n s _ n _ n t s!	vowels

The _____ sentence is easier to complete. You can see that _____ provide useful information.	second consonants
4. *Keywords* are examples of words containing common onset consonants. Letter–sound relationships for onset consonants are often taught with "keyword charts" of memorable words beginning with each of the initial _____.	consonants
5. The word *bell* is the keyword for the onset consonant _____. The word *cake* is the keyword for the onset consonant _____. The word *duck* is the keyword for the onset consonant _____. The word *fish* is the keyword for the onset consonant _____.	b c d f
6. These, and other, _____ consonants are included in phonics instruction.	onset

 Rime

Table 1 shows the most common rime patterns. These patterns, along with initial consonants and consonant combinations, are often included in the early part of phonics programs. Knowing these rime patterns helps young readers unlock the pronunciation of many words that they encounter. In fact, these 37 rime patterns account for 500 words that appear in beginning reading texts.

Table 1.

The 37 Most Common Rime Patterns

-a	-e	-i	-o	-u
(b)ack	(m)eat	(n)ice	(cl)ock	(d)uck
(m)ail	(b)ell	(st)ick	(j)oke	(r)ug
(r)ain	(cr)est	(w)ide	(sh)op	(j)ump
(c)ake		(l)ight	(st)ore	(j)unk
(s)ale		(w)ill	(n)ot	
(g)ame		(w)in		
(pl)an		(l)ine		
(b)ank		(br)ing		
(tr)ap		(th)ink		
(cr)ash		(tr)ip		
(c)at		(f)it		
(pl)ate				
(s)aw				
(st)ay				

This table is based on work initially conducted by Wylie and Durrell (1970).

7. From Table 1, you can see that the most frequent rime patterns begin with the vowel letter _____, and the least frequent rime patterns begin with the vowel letter _____.	a e
8. Two words that use the -ake rime pattern, begin with a single consonant, and are likely to be familiar to many first graders from their oral vocabulary would include _____ and _____.	bake, cake, fake, lake, make, rake, or take
9. Two words that use the -ot rime pattern, begin with a single consonant, and are likely to be familiar to many first graders from their oral vocabulary would include _____ and _____.	got, hot, lot, not, or pot
10. Rime patterns appear not only in words with one _____ but also in multiple-syllable words such as *lightning*.	syllable
11. Thus, onset–rime patterns are very helpful when decoding both _____ and words.	syllables
12. You will discover many different labels for rime patterns. These include terms such as *phonograms* and *word families*. Each term refers to common patterns containing a vowel and any following consonants within a single _____.	syllable

Consonant Patterns

Consonant Clusters

13. We have looked at single consonants appearing in the initial or what is called the _____ position. We should also recognize that multiple consonants might appear together at the beginning of words and syllables. These are called *consonant clusters*. Consonant clusters include two or three _____ that appear together, such as ch, th, st, str, bl, or pr.	onset consonants
14. There are two different types of consonant _____ that appear in the onset position (at the beginning) of words and syllables: consonant digraphs and consonant blends.	clusters

15. *Consonant digraphs* are two different _____ letters that appear together and represent a single sound, or phoneme, not usually associated with either letter. You do _____ hear elements of each, separate letter. Examples include <u>ch</u> (*child*), <u>ph</u> (*phone*), <u>sh</u> (*shop*), and <u>th</u> (*thin*).	consonant not
16. Can you identify the consonant digraphs in the following keywords? These are the most common consonant digraphs. The word *white* is the keyword for the consonant digraph _____. The word *chair* is the keyword for the consonant digraph _____. The words *this* and *thin* are the keywords for the consonant digraph _____. The word *shop* is the keyword for the consonant digraph _____. The word *phone* is the keyword for the consonant digraph _____.	 wh ch th sh ph
17. The consonant _____ <u>th</u> and <u>ch</u> each have several sounds.	digraphs
18. Let's look at the consonant digraph <u>th</u>. This digraph represents two different sounds: the voiced and voiceless <u>th</u> sound. Pronounce the words *this, that, their,* and *them.* The digraph _____ in these words is called the voiced <u>th</u> sound because we add voice to it when we say it. (Put your hand on your throat as you say each word, and you may feel the vibration of the voicing.)	 th
19. Pronounce the words *think* and *thin.* Hold one hand on your throat, and you will not feel any voicing when you say each word. The beginning sound in these words is different when compared to the _____ <u>th</u> sound. It is called the unvoiced, or voiceless, _____ sound.	 voiced th
20. The phoneme represented by <u>th</u> in *this* is the _____ <u>th</u> sound; the phoneme represented by <u>th</u> in *thin* is the unvoiced, or voiceless, _____ sound.	voiced th

21. As you pronounce the following words, indicate whether the <u>th</u> digraph is voiced or voiceless. *thank* _____ *the* _____ *thermos* _____ *thumb* _____ *these* _____	voiceless voiced voiceless voiceless voiced
22. Now let's look at the digraph <u>ch</u>. This consonant digraph represents three different sounds: the sound _____ as in *chair*, the sound _____ as in *character*, and the sound _____ as in *chef*.	/ch/ /k/ /sh/
23. Pronounce the words *character* and *chorus*. These words begin with the sound usually associated with the letter _____. <u>Ch</u> sometimes represents the sound associated with _____.	<u>k</u> <u>k</u>
24. Say the words *chef* and *chiffon*. These words begin with the sound usually associated with the digraph _____. *Chef, chiffon,* and *shoe* all sound the _____ in the onset position.	<u>sh</u> same
25. Let's summarize what we know about consonant digraphs appearing in the onset position. A consonant digraph is composed of _____ consonants that represent a single _____. Consonant digraphs include _____, _____, _____, _____, and _____. The onset digraph _____ may be voiced, as in *this*, or voiceless, as in *thin*. The onset digraph _____ may represent three different phonemes: the sounds often associated with <u>ch</u>, <u>k</u>, and <u>sh</u>.	two phoneme, <u>wh</u> <u>ch</u>, <u>th</u>, <u>sh</u> <u>ph</u>, <u>th</u> <u>ch</u>
26. Look at these words: *picture, phone,* and *pleasure*. Only one of these words has a consonant digraph in the onset position. That word is _____.	*phone*

27. A second type of consonant cluster appearing at the onset position is called a consonant _____. A *consonant blend* consists of two or three consecutive consonants, each representing a separate phoneme that is blended together.	blend
28. Here are several examples of consonant blends: *brick, blue, scream, skip,* and *street*. Notice how you can hear elements of each of the separate _____ as they are blended together.	phonemes
29. Identify the consonant blends in the onset position for these keywords. The word *blue* is the keyword for the consonant blend _____. The word *clown* is the keyword for the consonant blend _____. The word *flower* is the keyword for the consonant blend _____. The word *splash* is the keyword for the consonant blend _____. All of these consonant blends end with _____. Because of this, they are sometimes called the _____ blends.	bl cl fl spl l l
30. Now look at these keywords and identify the consonant blends in the onset position. The word *bread* is the keyword for the consonant blend _____. The word *crash* is the keyword for the consonant blend _____. The word *tree* is the keyword for the consonant blend _____. The word *three* is the keyword for the consonant blend _____. All of these consonant _____ end with _____. Because of this, they are sometimes called the r _____.	br cr tr thr blends, r blends

31. Now look at these keywords and identify the consonant blends in the onset position. The word *scale* is the keyword for the consonant blend _____.	sc
The word *skate* is the keyword for the consonant blend _____.	sk
The word *sled* is the keyword for the consonant blend _____.	sl
The word *spring* is the keyword for the consonant blend _____.	spr
The word *squirrel* is the keyword for the consonant blend _____.	squ
The word *string* is the keyword for the consonant blend _____.	str
All of these consonant blends _____ with _____.	begin, <u>s</u>
Because of this, they are sometimes called the _____ blends.	<u>s</u>
32. The three main categories of _____ blends are	consonant
(1) those with _____ as the final letter, (2) those with	<u>l</u>
_____ as the beginning letter, and (3) those with	<u>s</u>
_____ as the final letter.	<u>r</u>
33. As you have just learned, a consonant _____ is a	blend
combination of two or three _____ letters, each of which	consonant
retains its own _____ when pronounced.	phoneme (sound)

■ Special Consonant Patterns

34. The following _____ letters can represent more than one sound when they appear in certain contexts: <u>c</u>, g, <u>s</u>, <u>q</u>, <u>d</u>, <u>x</u>, <u>t</u>, and z. Many of these patterns are presented in reading programs	consonant
when _____ is taught. As a result, we will cover them here.	phonics

35. First, let's look at the single onset consonants c and g because they follow a similar pattern. Look at the two lists below and see if you can determine the two sounds of c in the onset position.

A	B
come	city
cow	celery
capture	cycle
cut	cymbal

All words in list A begin with the same sound. The sound in the onset position in list A is called the "hard c" sound; this sound is often represented by the letter _____ in words such as *kite*. Notice, too, the three vowels that follow c in each word in list A. These vowels are _____, _____, and _____.

k

o, a

u

36. Now let's look at a few other words beginning with the letter c and also followed by the vowels o, a, or u: *comb, cone, cat, can, cucumber*, and *cute*. These words follow the pattern because the onset letter c is pronounced like the _____ sound when followed by the vowels _____, _____, or _____. We refer to this as the "_____ c" sound.

k

o, a

u, hard

37. All words in list B begin with what we call the "soft c" sound. This is the sound represented by the letter s in words such as *sale*. Notice the three _____ that follow c in each word in list B. These vowels are _____, _____, and _____.

vowels

i, e

y

38. Now let's look at a few other words beginning with the letter c followed by the vowels i, e, or y: *circle, circus, center, cent, cylinder*, and *cypress*. These words also follow this pattern because the onset letter c is pronounced like the _____ sound when it is followed by the vowels _____, _____, or _____. We refer to this as the "_____ c" sound.

s

i

e, y

soft

39. You can see that the letter–sound relationship for the onset letter c is fairly regular. The pronunciation of this letter is usually determined by the _____ that follows it.

vowel

40. Now we can state the rule about letter–sound relationships that is often true for the onset letter <u>c</u>.

The onset letter <u>c</u> usually represents the sound associated with the letter <u>k</u> when it is followed by the vowels _____, _____, or _____. We refer to this as the "_____ c" sound.

The onset letter <u>c</u> usually represents the sound associated with <u>s</u> when it is followed by the vowels _____, _____, or _____. We refer to this as the "_____ c" sound.

<u>o</u>

<u>a</u>, <u>u</u>

hard

<u>e</u>, <u>y</u>

<u>i</u>, soft

41. The onset consonant g has a letter–sound relationship that patterns itself like the letter <u>c</u>. Look at the following two lists and see if you can determine the two sounds of g in the onset position.

C	*D*
good	giraffe
goat	gentle
game	gem
gun	gym

All words in list C begin with the sound most commonly associated with the onset consonant g. This is called the "hard g" sound. Notice the three vowels that follow g in each word in list C. These vowels are _____, _____, and _____.

<u>o</u>, <u>a</u>

<u>u</u>

42. Now let's look at a few other words beginning with the letter g and followed by the vowels <u>o</u>, <u>a</u>, or <u>u</u>: *go, gone, gate, gas, guppy,* and *guy*. These words also follow the pattern because the onset letter g is pronounced like the _____ sound when it is followed by the vowels _____, _____, or _____. We refer to this as the "_____ g" sound.

g

<u>o</u>, <u>a</u>

<u>u</u>, hard

43. All words in list D begin with what we call the "soft g" sound. This is the sound represented by the letter <u>j</u> in words such as *jam*. Notice the three _____ letters that follow g in each word in list D. These vowels are _____, _____, and _____.

vowel

<u>i</u>, <u>e</u>

<u>y</u>

44. Now let's look at a few other words beginning with the letter g followed by the vowels i, e, or y: *giant, germ, genius, gypsy,* and *gyrate.* These words also follow this pattern because the onset letter g is pronounced like the _____ sound when it is followed by the vowels _____, _____, or _____. We refer to this as the "_____ g" sound.	j i, e y, soft
45. Now we can state the rule about the letter–sound relationships that is often true for the onset letter _____. The onset letter g usually represents the sound associated with g when it is followed by the vowels _____, _____, or _____. We refer to this as the "_____ g" sound. The onset letter g usually represents the sound associated with the letter j when it is followed by the vowels _____, _____, or _____. We refer to this as the "_____ g" sound.	g o, a u, hard i e, y soft
46. S is another _____ with letter–sound relationships that pattern themselves in somewhat regular ways. The sound most commonly associated with s is represented by the s in the keyword *sock.* Pronounce the words *runs, his,* and *boys.* What letter usually represents the last sound that you hear in these words? _____ Using the letter s to represent the sound associated with the letter z is not taught as often as is the more common letter–sound association for s because s is more _____ in the onset position. For plurals or verb forms where s appears at the end of words, there are usually context or word-form clues that make knowing the letter–sound association less important.	consonant z common
47. The s appearing in the _____ position in words such as *sun, sit,* or *sing* represents the most common sound for this letter.	onset
48. The s appearing at the end of the words *his, runs,* and *boys* represents the sound often associated with the letter _____.	z

49. Complete the following generalizations related to sounds represented by the letter <u>s</u>: When the letter <u>s</u> appears in the _____ position, it represents the most common sound for <u>s</u>, the sound that appears at the beginning of the word *sun*. When <u>s</u> appears at the _____ of a word, it represents one of two sounds, either the sound usually associated with the letter _____ or the sound usually represented by the letter _____.	onset end s z
50. <u>T</u> is another consonant that represents several different _____. You know that the sound represented by the letter <u>t</u> is the sound heard in the keyword *turtle*. However, in combination with certain other letters, <u>t</u> can represent other sounds.	sounds
51. Pronounce the words *celebration*, *location*, and *vacation*. What are the last four letters in each word? _____	<u>tion</u>
52. Complete the following generalization: In the suffix _____, the letter <u>t</u> represents the sound of the digraph _____.	<u>tion</u> <u>sh</u>
53. Now look at another pattern for <u>t</u>. Pronounce the words *virtue*, *virtuous*, and *mutual*. The sound represented by <u>t</u> in these words is usually associated with the letters _____. In each case, the letter following <u>t</u> is _____.	<u>ch</u> <u>u</u>
54. Complete the following generalization: When the letter <u>t</u> is followed by the letter _____, it sometimes represents the sound associated with the consonant digraph _____	<u>u</u> <u>ch</u>
55. <u>X</u> is another consonant that represents several sounds. The common sound associated with the letter <u>x</u> is the same sound heard at the end of the word *books*. Thus, it can be said that the most common sound for the letter <u>x</u> represents the sounds associated with the letters _____.	<u>ks</u>

56. Pronounce the words *exist*, *examine*, and *exhibit*. The letter _____ in these words represents the sounds associated with the letters g̱ẕ.	x̱
57. Here is another sound that the letter x̱ sometimes represents. Pronounce the words *xylophone* and *xenon*. What letter usually represents the sound associated with x̱ in these words? _____ Where is the x̱ in *xylophone* and *xenon*? _____	ẕ onset (at the beginning)
58. Complete the following generalization: When the letter x̱ appears in the _____ position, it usually represents the sound associated with _____.	onset ẕ
59. The common sound associated with ḏ is heard in the keyword *dog*. Say the words *gradual*, *educate*, and *individual*. The letter _____ usually represents the sound of the underlined letter. The letter _____ follows the underlined ḏ in each word.	j̱ u̱
60. Complete the following generalization: When ḏ is followed by the vowel _____ in the middle of a word, it sometimes represents the sound associated with the letter _____.	u j̱

■ **Silent Consonant Patterns**

61. You have learned that some consonants represent more than one _____. You should also know that there are situations in which some consonants do not represent sounds but serve as markers for certain language patterns. The common terminology is *silent letter*.	sound
62. Look at the words *tall*, *off*, and *miss*. In each word, there is a _____ consonant. In the spoken word *tall*, there is _____ sound represented by the letter ḻ. In the spoken word *off*, there is _____ sound represented by the letter f̱. In the spoken word *miss*, there is _____ sound represented by the letter s̱.	double one one one

63. Complete the following generalization: When there is a double consonant in a word, usually only _____ of the consonants is heard.	one
64. Pronounce the words *knife, know,* and *knight.* What letter usually represents the first sound in these words? _____ The first two letters in each word are _____. Because <u>k</u> is _____, it can be called a _____ letter in this spelling pattern.	n kn silent, silent
65. Complete the following generalization: When a word or syllable starts with the letters <u>kn</u>, the _____ is _____.	k, silent
66. Pronounce the words *gnat, gnaw,* and *gnome.* What letter usually represents the first sound in these words? _____ The first two letters in each word are _____. The <u>g</u> is _____, or a marker.	n gn silent
67. Complete the following generalization: When a word or syllable starts with the letters <u>gn</u>, the _____ is _____.	g, silent (or a marker)
68. Pronounce the words *wrong, write,* and *wreath.* The letter that represents the first sound in these words is _____. What letter is silent (or a marker)? _____ When a word or syllable starts with <u>wr</u>, the _____ is silent, or a marker.	r w w
69. In the preceding examples, three consonant combinations that contain a silent letter or marker are _____, _____, and _____. In each of these letter combinations, the first of the two consonants is _____.	kn gn, wr silent (or a marker)
70. Pronounce the words *dumb, climb,* and *comb.* What letter represents the final sound in these words? _____ What letter follows the <u>m</u>? _____ The letter <u>b</u> is _____	m b silent

71. Complete the following generalization: When <u>b</u> is preceded by <u>m</u>, the _____ is _____, or a marker.	<u>b</u>, silent
72. Look at the words *doubt* and *debt*. What are the last two letters? _____ Which of the last two letters is silent, or a marker? _____	<u>bt</u> <u>b</u>
73. Complete the following generalization: When the letters <u>bt</u> appear together, the _____ is silent, or a marker.	<u>b</u>
74. Letter combinations in which <u>b</u> does not represent a sound are _____ and _____.	<u>mb</u>, <u>bt</u>
75. Look at the words *high, might,* and *fight.* What three consecutive letters do you see in each of the above words? _____ Pronounce each word. What letter represents the last sound in *high*? _____	<u>igh</u> <u>i</u>
76. Complete the following generalization: When the letters <u>igh</u> appear together, the _____ and the _____ are usually _____ and the vowel has a long <u>i</u> sound.	<u>g</u> <u>h</u>, silent (or a marker)
77. Look at the words *fetch, itch,* and *catch.* What three consecutive letters do you see in each of these words? _____ Pronounce each word. Which of the three letters in the <u>tch</u> combination does not represent a sound? _____	<u>tch</u> <u>t</u>
78. Complete the following generalization: When the letters <u>tch</u> appear together, the letter _____ is usually _____.	<u>t</u> silent (a marker)

79. In addition to the generalizations stated previously, there are other situations in which some consonants do not represent sounds. The following words illustrate some other examples of consonants that do not represent sounds. Pronounce each word and indicate the consonant that does not represent a sound:	
whole _____	<u>w</u>
hour _____	<u>h</u>
khaki _____	<u>h</u>
rhubarb _____	<u>h</u>
folk _____	<u>l</u>
calm _____	<u>l</u>
psychology _____	<u>p</u>
island _____	<u>s</u>
80. Letters in English do not always represent a single _____; nevertheless, knowing the more regular letter–sound relationships helps us to recognize many of the _____ we encounter. Understanding the basic elements of phonic knowledge is especially important for teachers of beginning readers.	sound words

✓ **SELF-CHECK FOR CHAPTER 3**

1. In English, the most consistent letter–sound relationships occur with _____.	consonants
2. Onset patterns appear at the _____ of words or syllables and consist of _____.	beginning consonants
3. Rime patterns appear at the _____ of syllables or words and begin with a _____.	end vowel
4. Onset and rime patterns combine to form _____ or _____.	words syllables
5. Consonant clusters include two or three consonants that appear _____.	together

6. The letters <u>ch</u> in the word *choose* are called a consonant _____ because it contains two consecutive consonants that represent a _____ sound, not usually associated with either letter.	digraph single
7. The letters <u>sk</u> in the word *skip* are called a consonant _____ because it contains two consecutive consonants, each representing a separate _____ that is blended together with the other.	blend phoneme
8. The onset letter <u>c</u> usually represents the sound associated with the letter <u>k</u> when it is followed by the vowels _____, _____, or _____. We refer to this as the "_____ c" sound.	<u>a</u> <u>o</u>, <u>u</u> hard
9. The onset letter g usually represents the sound associated with the letter j when it is followed by the vowels _____, _____, or _____. We refer to this as the "_____ g" sound.	<u>e</u> <u>i</u>, <u>y</u> soft
10. When there is a double consonant in a word, usually only one of the consonants is heard. The other is _____.	silent (or a marker)
11. When a word or syllable starts with the letters <u>kn</u>, <u>gn</u>, or <u>wr</u>, the _____ letter is usually _____.	first, silent (or a marker)

PRACTICAL EXAMPLES AND RESOURCES FOR TEACHING PHONICS (ONSET, RIME, AND CONSONANT PATTERNS) IN YOUR CLASSROOM

Take a Look Videos

Take a look at this video that shows you how to use onset and rime cubes to help students practice this important element of phonics, or graphophonics: http://bit.ly/1yqyUAT. One cube has all onset letters written on it and the other cube has all rimes. When students roll them, different combinations appear and they practice reading them. This is a wonderful activity for your class to play in small groups or individually.	

Take a look at this video that uses an engaging song to illustrate works with silent k: http://bit.ly/1uQcqYB.

Use it in your classroom, with a projector, to introduce silent k words to your class.

Take a look at this video that explains where several types of silent letters come from as English borrowed words from abroad: http://bit .ly/1zrN9cU.

Use it in your classroom for somewhat older students who may be struggling with reading.

 ## Lesson Suggestions

Whole-to-Parts Phonics Instruction: Teaching Letter–Sound Correspondences (http://bit.ly/1621Ya3).
This *ReadWriteThink* lesson is designed to teach letter–sound correspondences using onsets and rhymes after reading a selection of children's literature.

Word Wizards: Students Making Words (http://bit.ly/1DuBo4C).
Students look for and manipulate letter patterns within words using themes from four popular children's books. The lesson has both offline and online components.

Consonant Digraph Bingo (http://bit.ly/1LARyPu).
This lesson provides printable bingo cards for playing a bingo-like game to develop awareness of consonants and consonant digraphs. Great fun!

The Role of Phonics in Reading Instruction.
International Literacy Association. (1997). Newark, DE: International Literacy Association. A position statement from the Board of Directors of the International Literacy Association. This position statement (under revision) includes suggestions for the teaching of phonics, written by outstanding researchers and professionals in the field. Check frequently at www.literacyworldwide.org/ for updated position statements and teaching suggestions.

 ## Apps for Classroom Use

Consonant Blends: http://bit.ly/1LDaSvx
    Current cost: $0.99
        Pick a consonant blend and then try to find the matching rime or word ending.

ABC Phonics Rhyming Words Lite: http://bit.ly/1ytL7Vo

    Current cost: $2.99

        Engaging activities for learning onset and rime patterns.

Looney Tunes Phonics: http://bit.ly/165ys3j

    Current cost: $6.99 per grade level

        A comprehensive set of activities in phonics using Looney Tune characters.

iSort Words: http://bit.ly/1zv8imk

    Current cost: $3.99

        Many activities to learn common onset and rime patterns.

 ## Online Reading Resources

To learn more about phonics, explore these online resources:

- Linan-Thompson, S., & Vaughn, S. (2007). Phonics and word study. In *Research-based methods of reading instruction for English language learners, Grades K-4*. ASCD. (This online chapter presents a thorough discussion of effective phonics instruction, especially in relation to English Learners.)

  Retrieved from http://bit.ly/1DwkO4s

- Rasinski, T. (2000). Making and writing words using letter patterns. *Reading Online*. (A description of an important instructional practice to use in your classroom for teaching word recognition.)

  Retrieved from http://bit.ly/1yjBsQ7

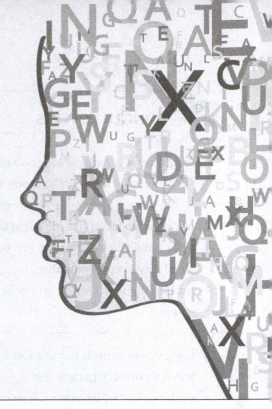

4

Phonics: Vowel Patterns

 INTRODUCTION

Our exploration of phonic knowledge continues with a discussion of the letter–sound relationships for vowels. The first section will explore letter–sound relationships between single vowels and vowel clusters. The second section will explore additional vowel generalizations. These relationships are often determined by where a vowel appears in a word. You will discover that the position of a vowel within a spelling pattern often provides more clues about its sound than does knowledge of letter–sound relationships. Regional speech patterns also influence the pronunciation of vowel phonemes, as do the pronunciation patterns that English Learners bring from their first language.

 VOWEL PATTERNS: AN INTERACTIVE TUTORIAL

1. Every syllable contains a vowel sound. Vowels are sounds produced without a restriction in the airstream. Five letters are often associated with vowel sounds: <u>a</u>, <u>e</u>, _____, _____, and _____. In addition, the letters <u>y</u> and <u>w</u> sometimes represent _____ sounds.	<u>i</u> <u>o</u>, <u>u</u> vowel
2. Letter–sound relationships for vowels closely follow the categories used for _____. Thus, there are single vowels as well as vowel clusters.	consonants

3. Single vowels include long vowels, short vowels, r-controlled vowels, and y when it functions as a single _____.	vowel
4. A long vowel sound is identical to the vowel names of the traditional vowel letters: a, e, i, o, and u. Thus, the vowel in the word *mine* represents the _____, or glided, vowel sound for i. In the word *make*, you hear a long, or glided, _____ sound.	long a
5. Long vowel sounds occur most frequently in two positions: (1) when a vowel occurs at the _____ of a word or syllable, such as *me, no, pa*-per, *ce*-dar, and *ci*-der, and (2) when a vowel is followed by a consonant and the letter e at the end of a _____, such as *mane, time, rope,* and *cute*. The final e in this pattern is usually _____.	end word silent (or a marker)
6. Each of the five traditional vowel letters also represents a short, or unglided, vowel sound. These _____ vowel sounds are often learned along with a set of keywords: a as in *apple*, e as in *egg*, i as in *ink*, o as in *octopus*, and u as in *umbrella*.	short
7. Short _____ sounds occur most frequently in a word or syllable that ends in a consonant or consonant cluster, such as *hap*-py, *let, win, ot*-ter, or *fun*.	vowel
8. Now look at this set of keywords for both long and short vowel identification. *Apple* is the keyword for the _____ sound of a. *Apron* is the keyword for the _____ sound of a. *Egg* is the keyword for the _____ sound of e. *Eleven* is the keyword for the _____ sound of e. *Ink* is the keyword for the _____ sound of i. *Ice* is the keyword for the _____ sound of i. *Octopus* is the keyword for the _____ sound of o. *Oat* is the keyword for the _____ sound of o. *Umbrella* is the keyword for the _____ sound of u. *Use* is the keyword for the _____ sound of u.	short long short long short long short long short long

9. When a vowel is followed by <u>r</u>, the <u>r</u> influences the vowel sound. These sounds are called _____-controlled vowel sounds. They are neither long nor short but have a sound determined largely by the following <u>r</u>.

r

Keywords for identifying <u>r</u>-controlled vowel sounds are as follows:
Car is the keyword for the vowel sound of _____.

<u>ar</u>

Her is the keyword for the vowel sound of _____.

<u>er</u>

Bird is the keyword for the vowel sound of _____.

<u>ir</u>

For is the keyword for the vowel sound of _____.

<u>or</u>

Turn is the keyword for the vowel sound of _____.

<u>ur</u>

Note that three of these sounds will be identical in many dialects. Which three graphemes do you think are often used to designate the same phoneme in many dialects? _____, _____, and _____.

<u>er</u>
<u>ir</u>, <u>ur</u>

10. The letter <u>y</u> may function as a single consonant or a single vowel. <u>Y</u> functions as a vowel when it appears in two positions. <u>Y</u> functions as a vowel when it appears at the end of a word with more than _____ syllable, such as *sandy*, *baby*, or *sixty*. In this case, <u>y</u> often represents the _____ sound of the letter <u>e</u>. <u>Y</u> also functions as a vowel when it appears at the end of a word with only one syllable. In this case, <u>y</u> usually represents the long sound for the letter _____, such as *try*, *my*, or *cry*.

one

long

i

11. For the following list of words, identify the vowel sounds as long, short, or <u>r</u>-controlled.

ape	_____	long <u>a</u>
far	_____	r-controlled <u>a</u>
we	_____	long <u>e</u>
nice	_____	long <u>i</u>
sly	_____	long <u>i</u>
fir	_____	r-controlled <u>i</u>
sticky	_____ and _____	short <u>i</u> and long <u>e</u>
fan	_____	short <u>a</u>
mute	_____	long <u>u</u>
met	_____	short <u>e</u>
try	_____	long <u>i</u>
tin	_____	short <u>i</u>
on	_____	short <u>o</u>

VOWEL CLUSTERS

12. Like consonants, vowels also appear in clusters. Vowel _____ consist of two or three vowel letters that often appear together, such as <u>ou</u>, <u>ee</u>, <u>ai</u>, and <u>oy</u>. There are two types of vowel clusters: vowel digraphs and vowel blends.	clusters

Vowel Digraphs

13. Two vowels appearing together that represent a single _____ are called vowel _____.	phoneme, digraphs
14. The following keywords are examples of the most common vowel _____.	digraphs
Meet is the keyword for the vowel digraph _____.	<u>ee</u>
Ceiling is the keyword for the _____ digraph _____.	vowel,
	<u>ei</u>
Toe is the keyword for the vowel _____ _____.	digraph, <u>oe</u>
Pie is the keyword for the vowel digraph _____.	<u>ie</u>
Easy is the keyword for the vowel digraph _____.	<u>ea</u>
Rain is the keyword for the vowel digraph _____.	<u>ai</u>
Boat is the keyword for the _____ digraph _____.	vowel
	<u>oa</u>
Play is the keyword for the vowel digraph _____.	<u>ay</u>
Grow is the keyword for the vowel digraph _____.	<u>ow</u>
Pronounce each keyword. Note that the previous vowel _____ all result in a _____ vowel sound. These can then be called _____ vowel _____.	digraphs, long
	long, digraphs

Vowel Blends (Diphthongs)

15. Vowel blends are a second type of vowel cluster. Vowel blends are two vowel letters that appear together and represent a blending of the sounds often associated with each letter, such as <u>oi</u> (*soil*), <u>oy</u> (*toy*), or <u>ou</u> (*mouse*). Listen to each of these vowel blends as you say them. In each vowel blend, you can hear elements of each vowel _____ blended together. Some people refer to vowel blends by another name—*diphthongs*.	sound

16. Here are the keywords for vowel blends or _____:	diphthongs
Oil is the keyword for the diphthong _____.	<u>oi</u>
Boy is the keyword for the diphthong _____.	<u>oy</u>
Cow is the keyword for the diphthong _____.	<u>ow</u>
Out is the keyword for the diphthong _____.	<u>ou</u>
Note that each diphthong includes _____ letters and the blended sounds represented by each one.	two
17. *Oil* and *boy* contain the same vowel sound. *Cow* and *out* contain the same _____ sound. Therefore, <u>oy</u> and _____ represent the same vowel _____, and <u>ou</u> and _____ represent the same _____ sound.	vowel, <u>oi</u> sound <u>ow</u>, vowel
18. Let's summarize. Digraphs and diphthongs are two types of _____ clusters. Each is composed of _____ vowels. A digraph represents _____ sound. A diphthong represents a blend of _____ vowel sounds within a single syllable. Indicate if the following words contain digraphs or diphthongs:	vowel, two one two
pout _____	diphthong
toy _____	diphthong
snow _____	digraph
clout _____	diphthong
coat _____	digraph
read _____	digraph
how _____	diphthong

VOWEL GENERALIZATIONS

19. Letter–sound relationships for vowels are often determined by their locations within words and syllables. These locations are often labeled by the pattern of consonants (C) and vowels (V) that exist. Thus, a <u>CVC</u> pattern represents a vowel that appears in a word or syllable surrounded by two _____, such as the word *hot*. A <u>CV</u> pattern represents a word or syllable in which the vowel appears at the _____ of a word or syllable, such as the word *me*. The following generalizations, like most other phonic rules, do not apply all the time. Nevertheless, familiarity with these patterns may often assist children who are unable to recognize an unfamiliar word.	consonants end

Vowel Generalization 1 (<u>CVC</u> or <u>VC</u>)

20. Look at the following single-syllable words: *get bag fun rid hot at is* In each word, there is _____ vowel. The final letter in each word is a _____.	one consonant
The <u>e</u> in *get* represents the _____ <u>e</u> phoneme.	short
The <u>a</u> in *bag* represents the _____ <u>a</u> phoneme.	short
The <u>u</u> in *fun* represents the _____ <u>u</u> phoneme.	short
The <u>i</u> in *rid* represents the short _____ sound.	<u>i</u>
The <u>o</u> in *hot* represents the short _____ sound.	<u>o</u>
The <u>i</u> in *is* represents the short _____ sound.	<u>i</u>
21. Complete the following generalization: In single-syllable words, when there is _____ vowel in a word and the word ends in a _____, the vowel usually represents the _____ vowel sound.	one consonant short
Here's another way of stating this generalization: The vowel is usually _____ when a single-syllable word ends in a _____.	short consonant

Vowel Generalization 2 (<u>CV</u>)

22. Look at the following words: *go he hi me* In each of these words, there is _____ vowel. That vowel is at the _____ of the word.	one end
The <u>o</u> in *go* represents the long <u>o</u> _____.	sound
The <u>e</u> in *he* represents the long _____ sound.	<u>e</u>
The <u>i</u> in *hi* represents the _____ <u>i</u> sound.	long
The <u>e</u> in *me* represents the long _____ sound.	<u>e</u>
23. Complete the following generalization: When the only vowel in a word is at the _____ of the word, the vowel usually represents the _____ vowel sound.	end long

24. Here's another way of stating this generalization: The vowel sound is usually _____ when the vowel is the _____ letter in the word.	long final (or last)

Vowel Generalization 3 (VCE)

25. Look at the following words: *ride rope make use* There are _____ vowels in each word. The last letter in each word is _____. The final <u>e</u> is separated from the first vowel by _____ consonant. The <u>i</u> in *ride* represents the long _____ sound. The <u>o</u> in *rope* represents the long _____ sound. The <u>a</u> in *make* represents the _____ a sound. The first vowel in *use* represents the long _____ sound. The final <u>e</u> in *ride, rope, make,* and *use* is _____. The final <u>e</u> can be considered a marker for this spelling pattern.	two e one i o long u silent
26. Complete the following generalization: When a word has two vowels, one of which is a final _____, separated from the first vowel by one consonant, the first vowel usually has a _____ sound, and the <u>e</u> is usually _____.	e long, silent (or a marker)
27. Here's another way of stating this generalization: The final <u>e</u> is usually _____, indicating that the preceding vowel has a _____ sound in words where the final <u>e</u> and preceding vowel are separated by _____ consonant.	silent (or a marker) long one

Vowel Generalization 4 (VV)

28. Look at the following words: *rain eat boat play meet* In each word, there are _____ vowels. The pattern of two consecutive vowels gives a clue to the expected vowel sound. Pronounce the word *rain*. You hear the _____ _____ sound. The <u>i</u> is _____. The second vowel is a marker for this spelling pattern.	two long a, silent

Pronounce the word *eat*. You hear the _____ _____ sound. The <u>a</u> is _____.	long e, silent (or a marker)
Boat has a _____ <u>o</u> and a _____ <u>a</u>.	long, silent (or a marker)
Play has a _____ <u>a</u> and a _____ <u>y</u>.	long, silent (or a marker)
Meet has a _____ <u>e</u> and a _____ <u>e</u>.	long, silent (or a marker)
29. Common double vowel combinations that usually result in a long sound are <u>ai</u>, _____, <u>oa</u>, <u>ay</u>, and _____.	ea, ee
30. Complete the following generalization: When there are two consecutive vowels in a word, the first one usually has a _____ sound, and the second one is usually _____, unless they are vowel diphthongs.	long silent (or a marker)
31. Here's another way of stating this generalization: A _____ vowel sound is usually produced when two vowels appear side by side. The vowel sound heard is the long _____ of the first vowel; the second vowel is _____ (or a marker), unless the two vowels are vowel _____.	long sound silent diphthongs

☑ **SELF-CHECK FOR CHAPTER 4**

1. You have noticed that a vowel may have a long _____ in three contexts.	sound
(a) A word that ends in <u>e</u> preceded by a _____ consonant usually has a _____ sound for the first vowel.	single long
(b) When there are two consecutive vowels, the _____ vowel is usually long, and the second one is silent (or a marker), unless the two vowels are a _____.	first diphthong
(c) When the only vowel comes at the _____ of a syllable or word, that vowel is usually long.	end
2. Short vowel sounds appear in a syllable or word that ends in a _____ or a consonant cluster.	consonant
3. <u>R</u>-controlled vowels are neither long nor _____. They have a sound determined by the _____ that follows them.	short r

4. Y represents the long _____ sound when it appears at the end of a word with more than two syllables. Y has the long _____ sound when it appears at the end of a word with only one syllable.	e i
5. There are two types of vowel clusters: vowel _____ and vowel _____ or diphthongs.	digraphs blends
6. A digraph represents _____ sound. A _____ represents a blend of two vowel sounds.	one, blend (diphthong)
7. A vowel usually represents the _____ sound when a single-syllable word ends in a _____.	short consonant
8. When the only vowel in a word appears at the end, the vowel is usually _____.	long
9. When a word has two vowels, one of which is a final e, separated from the first vowel by one consonant, the first vowel usually represents the _____ sound, and the _____ is usually silent.	long, e
10. A _____ vowel sound is usually produced when two vowels appear side by side. The first vowel represents the _____ sound, and the second vowel is usually _____.	long long, silent (or a marker)

PRACTICAL EXAMPLES AND RESOURCES FOR TEACHING PHONICS (VOWEL PATTERNS) IN YOUR CLASSROOM

Take a Look Videos

Take a look at this video that shows a technique for helping students blend short vowel sounds appearing in the middle of single-syllable words: http://bit.ly/1LEpkU4.

As the teacher places the individual letters closer together, she shows students how to sound out the individual letter sounds quickly together.

Take a look at this video: http://bit.ly/1z6yWBv.

It can be used as a cute video introduction to the silent <u>e</u> rule in your class.

Take a look at this video: http://bit.ly/1D6m3sR.

It provides a vocal video introduction to the five main vowel letters.

 Lesson Suggestions

Teaching Short-Vowel Discrimination Using Dr. Seuss Rhymes (http://bit.ly/1DxpmaN).

This lesson uses contrasting short-vowel patterns to support first- and second-grade students' use of analogy to apply their knowledge of vowel sounds in reading and spelling new words. Students discover patterns in words, sort words based on their vowel patterns, and apply their knowledge in reading and writing activities.

Picture Match (http://bit.ly/1EZO5FN).

This lesson provides practice with identifying beginning-letter and short- and long-vowel sounds through a simple, online game. Great fun!

The Two Voices of the <u>ow</u> *Spelling Pattern* (http://bit.ly/1yvqMyR).

This lesson can be used as part of a series of lessons and modified for other vowel patterns. It is designed to show students how each vowel in the English alphabet represents a different set of sounds when used in different spelling patterns.

Long Vowel / Short Vowel Lesson Plans (http://bit.ly/1vp3Q94).

These lesson plans include a wide variety of activities and lesson plans for teaching long and short vowels. They also have links to some commercially available materials, but most activities are free and include downloadable materials.

 Apps for Classroom Use

Phonics Vowels—Short Vowels, Long Vowels, Two Vowels: http://bit.ly/1D6bjeb

Current cost: $3.95

Teaches an extensive set of vowel sounds and vowel combinations through a game context.

Tiki Bear Phonics HD—Vowel Sounds: http://apple.vshare.com/387209739.html

   Current cost: Free

      Designed for younger children, this app teaches the basic vowel sounds.

ABC Phonics Word Family: http://bit.ly/1DxKo9c

   Current cost: Free

      Provides activities with a variety of early phonics elements including vowel sounds.

 Online Reading Resources

To learn more about phonics, explore these online resources:

- Shanker, J. (2007). *Developing phonics knowledge: Blends, digraphs, and diphthongs*. (This short article provides a summary and guidelines for teaching vowel sounds to young children, including English Learners.)

   Retrieved from http://edcate.co/1LEU3Ac

- Ehri, L. C. (2003). *Systematic phonics instruction: Findings of the national reading panel*. (This article summarizes the research base in phonics and the utility of instruction in phonics.)

   Retrieved from http://files.eric.ed.gov/fulltext/ED479646.pdf

- Johnston, F. P. (2001). The utility of phonic generalizations: Let's take another look at Clymer's conclusions. *The Reading Teacher, 55*, 132–143. (This article summarizes the utility of many phonic generalizations including vowel patterns.)

   Retrieved from http://bit.ly/1D6qX9j

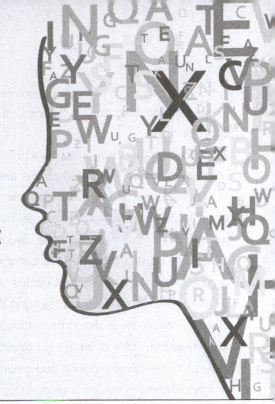

5

Context

INTRODUCTION

Readers use many strategies to identify and pronounce words that might be unfamiliar to them in print. Phonics is just one of these strategies. Often, words are in a reader's speaking or listening vocabulary, and context clues can be used to identify and pronounce these words. Context clues include using the surrounding information to help identify a word. Context is a very important aid to word analysis and comprehension. It helps to determine word pronunciation and meaning.

Context operates at many levels to help readers determine pronunciation. Usually, context refers to the text surrounding an unfamiliar word and includes language structure (*syntactic*) clues and meaning (*semantic*) clues. For example, if the first sentence in a paragraph was *John went to the* _____, the language structure provides a clue for the type of word (the part of speech) that is appropriate for the blank—in this case, a noun. But it does not indicate the exact word that belongs in the blank. If the first letters of the last word were given (e.g., *John went to the st*_____.), then readers might predict that the target word was *store* or *street*. They could then use other information in the paragraph to confirm or reject their predictions.

In addition to surrounding print, other context clues, such as images and other graphics, also provide help with meaning and pronunciation.

Predicting meaning and pronunciation are important aspects of using context clues.

Context applies not only to a whole word but also within word contexts. For example, readers can use knowledge of letter patterns to predict letters that appear within words, as well as their phonics knowledge. You know, for example, the letter most likely to follow q in English. A reader can also use discourse knowledge as a form of context to predict the ending to a story. For example, you can probably predict the end of a story that begins *Once upon a time. . . .*

In all cases, a reader's background knowledge interacts with context clues to help readers determine unfamiliar words. For example, knowing about how one pays for things in a store can help a reader to determine the pronunciation and meaning of *cashier*.

For children in the early elementary grades, words encountered in their reading materials are usually part of their listening and speaking vocabularies. Thus, using meaningful context is often a helpful word analysis strategy. Syntactic (or language patterning) clues and semantic (or meaning) clues function together with a reader's linguistic and experiential background knowledge. Readers integrate the clues from all these systems of language in the reading process.

 ## THE IMPORTANCE AND USE OF CONTEXT: AN INTERACTIVE TUTORIAL

1. When trying to determine the pronunciation and _____ of an unfamiliar word, readers can use several types of context clues.	meaning
2. Perhaps the most commonly used context is information surrounding an unfamiliar word. In addition, readers use their linguistic and _____ knowledge to help them with unfamiliar words. Pictures and knowing the story _____ are also important sources of context clues. This can be especially important for struggling readers or _____.	background (or prior) structure (or grammar) English Learners
3. Even when readers use strategies other than context, they often use context to check their efforts at pronunciation and see if the word makes _____.	sense

USING CONTEXT TO CHECK WORD ANALYSIS

4. Readers use context to determine whether their word analysis techniques were successful. For example, say the following word to yourself:

   object

   Even when readers apply appropriate phonics knowledge, the actual _____ can't be determined until the word is used in context. In which of the following sentences does the word you pronounced best fit?

   (a) I _____ to your insults.
   (b) The _____ of the game is to win.

   If your pronunciation was *ob'ject*, you would pick sentence _____. If your pronunciation was *ob ject'*, you would pick sentence _____. Neither pronunciation was right or wrong until it was checked within the _____ of the sentence.

   pronunciation

   (b)
   (a)
   context

5. As another example, let's imagine that you looked at the word *hoping* and pronounced it /hop/ing.

   Would that be correct? _____ The word should be pronounced _____ing.

   If you did not correctly recognize the pronunciation of the word and you checked the _____ from which the word came, you would probably be able to correct yourself.

   (a) Mary was *hoping* for a nice birthday present.

   no
   /hope/

   context

USING CONTEXT WITH OTHER WORD ANALYSIS TECHNIQUES

6. Context is used in combination with other word analysis strategies. Sometimes, vowel pronunciation generalizations can be used to predict the pronunciation, but the _____ must be used to confirm such pronunciations. At other times, context might predispose a reader toward a certain pronunciation, but pronunciation generalizations force a _____ in the prediction.

   context

   change

7. Read the following sentence:

    (a) I'm looking for some heavy metal. Please *lead* me to the *lead*.

    In this example, a vowel pronunciation generalization predicts that each word written as *lead* is pronounced _____ (see item 30 on page 47). However, context as a word analysis strategy indicates that the first instance of *lead* must be a verb, and the second instance must be a noun. A reader's linguistic knowledge _____ with context and the vowel pronunciation generalization to confirm the pronunciation /leed/ in the first instance and _____ in the second.

    /leed/

    interacts

    /led/

8. In the following sentence, context predicts a _____, and if unaware of the initial p, most readers predict the word *brother*.

    (a) Sarah, who was now six, had always wanted either a sister or a

    p_____.

    In this case, letter name knowledge interacts with context clues and the reader may predict *pet* using, in part, alphabetic and phonics knowledge, aided by _____.

    noun

    context

9. At times, however, linguistic context in surrounding print does not help to either confirm or suggest the meaning of a word, even though it indicates the part of speech. For example, read the following:

    (a) I always wanted a _____, and now I finally have one!
        My long wait for a _____ was over, and I was so happy!
        No longer would I be left out of the group.

    Even though linguistic context in the surrounding print predicts a _____, there are so many possibilities that context provided by the surrounding print is not helpful. However, if a picture were available, perhaps showing a just-opened present with someone happily holding the unwrapped item, then picture-based context would help narrow the possible _____. And, of course, a reader's phonics knowledge would be brought to bear on the word and _____ possibilities, as well.

    noun

    nouns

    constrain

10. Look also at the following example.

(a) I was told the *ethmoid* was broken. However, although it was painful, it was not life threatening.

This example shows that unless an word is already defined within a reader's _____ vocabulary, attempts at pronunciation might be correct but will not result in _____. (Did you know that *ethmoid* is a bone in your nose?)

oral (speaking)

meaning

USING CONTEXT AS A BASIC WORD ANALYSIS TECHNIQUE TO DETERMINE MEANING

11. Many authors intentionally provide context _____ for their readers. Special efforts are often made when new or difficult _____ are introduced. The following examples illustrate several of the more commonly used techniques.

clues

words (terms; concepts)

---

12. *Example 1:* Jim and Joan played a *set* of tennis. A set of tennis is completed when one player has won six or more games by a margin of two games.

In this example, the author has provided a _____ for the term _____ of tennis.

The technique of _____ words is usually limited to situations where the word is used for the first time in a passage.

definition

set

defining

---

13. *Example 2:* Many young children are *hyperopic*, or farsighted.

In this case, the author has provided a _____, *farsighted*, for the unfamiliar term.

_____ are used in the same manner as definitions when an author wants to explain a difficult word or concept.

synonym

Synonyms

14. *Example 3:* Suburban dwellers are seeing their communities grow ever more crowded, as they witness the development of a *megalopolis*. High-rise buildings, shopping centers and housing developments, schools, parks, museums, and medical facilities seem to appear constantly. For example, some areas between major cities are growing at a rate that predicts a continuous expanse of structures and people between cities that used to be separated by significant green space or natural environments.

In the above paragraph, readers can tell that a *megalopolis* is the continuous development of _____ areas.

metropolitan

Readers can use two clues. Their first clue is that the topic being discussed is related to suburban development. Their second clue is an _____.

example

15. *Example 4:* Reading aloud can cause *anguish* for some children. John, a boy of ten, suffered much embarrassment because he was shy and felt that he read poorly when reading aloud. He felt terrible, almost tortured, when asked to read aloud.

In example 4, clues are provided for the term *anguish* by an _____. In such cases, the author attempts to relate to an _____ that the reader can understand. Many authors find that using examples makes their writing more meaningful.

example
experience (event)

16. Example patterns are very helpful but often depend on a reader's _____ knowledge. The following sentence illustrates an _____ pattern:

background (prior)
example

(a) Europe, Asia, North America, South America, Africa, Australia, and Antarctica are the seven *continents*.

Note that while they can be useful, without appropriate background knowledge, an _____ pattern will not provide the context clues that are necessary to determine the target word.

example

17. *Example 5:* Many children came to Mary's birthday party. They played games, ate cake and ice cream, and sang "Happy Birthday" to Mary. She thought it was one of the best days of her life. She was *ecstatic*. In example 5, the mood of the story was the _____ to the meaning of *ecstatic*. *Ecstatic*, as used in the above context, means very happy. Readers might not know how to pronounce the word *ecstatic*, but they can come closer to an accurate meaning due to the _____ created by the story.	clue mood
18. Authors find many ways to help readers discover the meaning of words by providing _____ clues. The examples given previously provide some of the common types of context clues. Definition, example, _____, and _____ are common types of context clues.	context synonym, mood
19. To use context effectively, readers need to be flexible in using surrounding text. In the following example, the context clues are located _____ the target word. (a) The teenager had been swimming since she was an infant. It is not surprising that she is a really good *swimmer*.	before
20. Read the following sentence: (a) A *swimmer* is a person who swims. In this example, the context clues are located _____ the target word.	after
21. Context clues can also be provided by a _____ or an appositive phrase that follows the target word. For example, (a) He was *delayed*, or made late, because his car broke down. (b) The *jockey* (a person who rides racehorses) was very good at her job.	clause

22. Readers also use comparison patterns in using context to determine meaning and pronunciation. _____ patterns can also require that readers read past the target word or look _____ at what preceded it.	Comparison back
(a) The *ancient* rock formations were as old as the earth itself.	
(b) I hate going to bed early. In fact, I *despise* it.	
23. Read the following sentences and decide how context can help to determine the italicized target word.	
(a) My car is *quiet*, unlike the noisy thing that my brother drives!	
(b) Even though I was fond of Bill, I truly *loved* Bob.	
(c) It is *warm* during our winters, especially when compared to winter in Alaska.	
The above sentences illustrate _____ patterns that help readers to use context clues.	contrast

LIMITATIONS OF USING CONTEXT CLUES

24. From the previous examples, you probably noticed that context clues have more to do with meaning than with _____. It is possible that readers could use a synonym for an unfamiliar word when using _____ clues as their only form of word analysis. Other types of word _____ strategies, as discussed in other chapters, including knowledge of phonics, phonemic awareness, and the alphabetic principle, in _____ with context clues, add to accuracy.	pronunciation context analysis combination
25. *Example 6:* Mary had a birthday <predicted word would go here>. If asked for a predicted word, one might substitute words such as *today*, *party*, or *surprise*. However, because readers look closely at the initial consonant, when the example reads "Mary had a birthday *p*____," the reader's choices are limited. Now, of the words listed, only _____ will fit.	*party*

26. Readers might be able to supply a missing word in a sentence, but they might have a limited understanding of the word's _____ because they lack knowledge of the concept(s) that the word represents.	meaning
27. Using context _____ should not be considered as a substitute for a complete program of vocabulary development. The more extensive readers' speaking and _____ vocabularies are, the greater their resources are for using context clues.	clues listening
28. Authors do not always supply the needed clue. Therefore, if readers rely on using only _____, their word analysis strategies will not be as _____ as they could be.	context effective
29. Readers will find that they need to know the words, ideas, and pictures _____ an unfamiliar word to use context effectively, and authors provide many different _____ of context clues.	around (surrounding) types
30. Readers will also find _____ to be an effective means for checking other attempts at _____ analysis.	context word

✓ SELF-CHECK FOR CHAPTER 5

1. The following sentences contain language structure clues: (a) John _____ to the store. (b) The _____ is getting cold. In sentence (a), you know the word will be a _____. In sentence (b), you know the word will be a _____.	verb noun
2. Context clues can be used in the following ways: (a) as a technique to determine the _____ of an unfamiliar word (b) to check a pronounced word to see if the word makes _____ (c) as a step when using other _____ analysis strategies	meaning sense word

3. The types of patterns that readers find useful when applying context clues are _____ patterns, _____ patterns, and _____ patterns.

comparison, contrast

example

PRACTICAL EXAMPLES AND RESOURCES FOR TEACHING CONTEXT SKILLS IN YOUR CLASSROOM

Take a Look Videos

Take a look at this video that shows the use of context to discover word meanings: http://bit.ly/1C0mhPw.

Note, however, that the children can already pronounce (read) the words.

Take a look at this video of a rap/song: http://www.flocabulary.com/context-clues/.

This rap/song is about using context clues and serves as a reminder of many of the concepts discussed in this chapter.

Take a look at this video of a lesson using context clues: https://www.youtube.com/watch?v=oDO6jfhPGS4.

This is from a fourth-grade lesson.

Take a look at this video of a peer teaching lesson: https://www.youtube.com/watch?v=zsOwNmL4nQ8.

It shows a video of one child helping another to pronounce words from context.

Lesson Suggestions

Context Clues Lesson Plan (http://bit.ly/14FIOX1). This word detective game is designed to help students understand the various types of context clues that can appear during their reading.

Activating Strategies for Teaching Context Clues (http://bit.ly/1y18ydL). This lesson provides four useful activities for teaching the recognition of words in context.

Solving Word Meanings: Engaging Strategies for Vocabulary Development (http://bit.ly/1in1UQG). Includes lesson plans that deal specifically with introducing and practicing context clues. While the examples used are more appropriate for grades three and above, the steps can be easily modified for use with children in earlier grades.

Apps for Classroom Use

Minimod Basic Cloze Practice Lite: http://bit.ly/1y18n2d

    Current cost: $2.95

        A "lite" version of an App that provides practice in using context.

 Online Reading Resources

To learn more about context use during reading, explore these online resources:

- Fisher, D., Frey, N., & Lapp, D. (2012). Building and activating students' background knowledge: It's what they already know that counts. *Middle School Journal, 43*(3), 22–31.

  Retrieved from http://bit.ly/1CnzZjh

- Fries-Gaither, J. (2008). Teacher resources for making inferences, using context clues. *Beyond penguins and polar bears: An online magazine for K–5 teachers.* (2). (An article describing a variety of forms of context use during reading.)

  Retrieved from http://bit.ly/1C0E751

- Weaver, C., & Brown, J. (1996). Facts on the use of context in reading. (A short review on the use of context during word recognition and reading).

  Retrieved from http://bit.ly/17upSfF

6

Sight Words

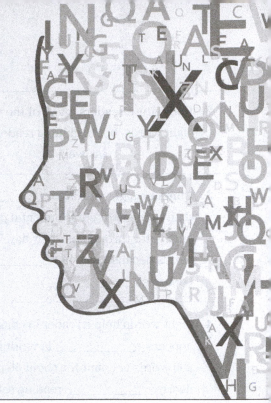

INTRODUCTION

Readers use a combination of word analysis strategies that are discussed throughout this book, but many words are recognized effortlessly and automatically. Such words are called *sight words* because they appear to be recognized and pronounced on sight, without any conscious application of decoding or word analysis strategies. Mature readers recognize most words that they encounter in print by relying on their sight word knowledge. They develop this ability over time through extensive reading experiences, initially relying on other, more conscious strategies, such as phonics. Beginning readers may recognize some words automatically, but they usually know relatively few words on sight as they read. Beginning readers will develop their sight word knowledge by being exposed to words in print and through extensive reading experiences. Through interaction with words in books and other settings, children will build sight word knowledge and a love of reading.

THE DEVELOPMENT OF SIGHT WORD KNOWLEDGE: AN INTERACTIVE TUTORIAL

1. Words that do not require the conscious use of word _____ strategies are called sight words. These words are recognized and pronounced automatically, seemingly on _____.

analysis	
sight	

2. For mature readers, most of the words that they encounter are sight words, but beginning readers usually have some sight word _____ as well.	knowledge
3. Common sight words for _____ readers often include their name and "environmental print" that children often encounter throughout their day. These words have become sight words because they have _____ for the child and have been seen _____.	beginning meaning often
4. Sight words help a reader because a fairly small set of words appears _____ in writing. In fact, approximately 200 words account for about 50 percent of the words in nearly _____ reading selection, and 400 words make up about 70 percent of most writing. These are called _____-frequency words.	frequently (or often) any high
5. Readers acquire most high-frequency words over time because they see these words very _____.	often
6. At first, however, beginning readers try to recognize and pronounce these words by using other word analysis strategies, such as _____ or a phonic strategy.	context
7. After repeated experiences with such words in meaningful context, these words become _____ words.	sight
8. Several people have provided lists of high-frequency words that appear in children's _____ materials. These lists can be helpful when teaching sight words to beginning _____.	reading readers
9. Perhaps the most well-known list is the *Dolch List of Basic Sight Words*. Recent analyses indicate that the _____ list accounts for about 50 percent of _____ in common K–3 reading material.	Dolch words

FIGURE 1 Dolch List of Basic Sight Words

a	did	have	me	said	try
	do	he	much	saw	two
about	does	help	must	say	
after	done	her	my	see	under
again	don't	here	myself	seven	up
all	down	him		shall	upon
always	draw	his	never	she	us
am	drink	hold	new	show	use
an		hot	no	sing	
and	eat	how	not	sit	very
any	eight	hurt	now	six	
are	every			sleep	walk
around		I	of	small	want
as	fall	if	off	so	warm
at	far	in	old	some	was
	fast	into	on	soon	wash
be	find	is	once	start	we
because	first	it	one	stop	well
been	five	its	only		went
before	fly		open	take	were
best	for	jump	or	tell	what
big	found	just	our	ten	when
black	four		out	thank	where
blue	from	keep	over	that	which
both	full	kind	own	the	white
bring	funny	know		their	who
brown			pick	them	why
but	gave	laugh	play	then	will
buy	get	let	please	there	wish
by	give	light	pretty	these	with
	go	like	pull	they	work
call	goes	little	put	think	would
came	going	live		this	write
can	good	long	ran	those	
carry	got	look	read	three	yellow
clean	green		red	to	yes
cold	grow	made	ride	today	you
come		make	right	together	your
could	had	many	round	too	
cut	has	may	run		

10. More recent lists have been compiled by Fry (2004), whose list of 1,000 Instant Words is also highly regarded as representative of high-_____ words in written English. See also Fry, Kress, and Fountoukidis (2006) for helpful lists of words useful in elementary and secondary grades.

frequency

11. Look at the words on the Dolch list in Figure 1. Why do you think this list has been so _____, over decades, in representing high-frequency words?

stable (reliable)

12. Did you notice that many of the words appearing on the list are mainly function words? Words such as *a, and, the, any, because,* and so on are used very _____, and their frequency of use has not changed through the years. It is not surprising, when looking at a high-frequency word list, that these words account for so _____ of the words found in a text.	frequently (often) many
13. Looking at the words on a high-frequency word list should give you some insight into the kinds of words that should be _____ as sight words.	taught

14. The words that should be taught as initial sight words have three important characteristics:
   (a) Words that should be _____ as initial sight words should appear frequently in print; they should be high-_____ words. A word such as *the*, as opposed to a word such as *monkey*, should be taught as sight words.
   (b) Words that should be taught as sight words should have meanings that are in a reader's oral _____. Words such as *car* and *home* are more appropriate than a word such as *turbine*.
   (c) Words that should be taught as initial sight words often cannot be recognized or pronounced by applying phonic _____. Teaching such words as sight words allows readers to recognize irregular words when they are encountered in print. Words such as *one, said,* and *some* are examples of such words.
	taught
	
	frequency
	
	vocabulary
	
	generalizations (rules)

15. Also, for all readers, but especially for English Learners who may not have high-frequency English words in their oral _____ vocabulary, sight words to be taught could come from high-interest materials that include words that are repeated _____ in the text. Words from such high-interest reading material can be provided in addition to the sight words and strategies discussed in this chapter.	English frequently (often)
16. Although sight word learning for beginning readers often involves words learned from high-frequency word lists and from their _____, most words become sight words through readers' repeated _____ with words in print.	environment interactions

17. Thus, a good program of sight word instruction will emphasize wide _____ as well as provide initial, direct instruction of sight words for beginning readers.	reading
18. Common strategies for developing sight word knowledge in young children include labeling common classroom items and creating word walls, where words are posted and referred to later. Such procedures help children see common words repeatedly and provide additional _____ print.	environmental
19. Another common strategy is modeled writing, where teachers can draw attention to _____ words during a writing activity that models writing behavior. In this way, teachers can merge several instructional goals within the modeled writing activity.	sight

✓ **SELF-CHECK FOR CHAPTER 6**

1. When a word is recognized and pronounced automatically, it is called a _____ _____.	sight, word
2. You should consider the following when choosing words to teach as sight words: (a) The words should appear _____ in print. (b) The words should be in a reader's _____ vocabulary. (c) The words cannot be pronounced using _____ generalizations.	frequently oral phonic
3. Most sight words are learned _____ by readers through their own _____ experiences.	independently reading
4. It is important to provide meaningful _____ experiences for beginning readers because this helps to develop _____ _____ knowledge.	reading sight, word

PRACTICAL EXAMPLES AND RESOURCES FOR TEACHING SIGHT WORDS IN YOUR CLASSROOM

 ### Take a Look Videos

Take a look at this video voice-over of examples of a word wall and other strategies: https://www.youtube.com/watch?v=dPBxankkkvM. It discusses sight words and high-frequency words near the beginning of the video and teaching word parts, such as syllables, later.

Take a look at this video by a K–3 teacher: https://www.youtube.com/watch?v=PSSbhgpOYDY.
She discusses how she teaches sight words to her students.

 ### Lesson Suggestions

Activities to Reinforce and Teach Sight Words (http://teachers.net/lessons/posts/485.html). This website presents whole-class and small-group activities that can be used to develop sight word knowledge.

Sight Word Soup (http://teachers.net/lessons/posts/56.html). This website provides a strategy to teach words from common sight word lists and later apply them.

Teaching Sight Words (http://www.readingresource.net/sightwords.html). This includes a list of activities to help students master sight words for use with individual or groups of children.

 ### Apps for Classroom Use

Sight Word List: Learn to Read Flash Cards and Games: http://bit.ly/1yEzcXl

Current cost: Free

A "flash card" app that presents the Dolch Word lists, by level, for use as a practice activity.

Play Sight Words: Gr. 1 & 2: http://bit.ly/1yEzcXl

Current cost: Free

Includes several games to develop and practice sight words.

Eggy 250 HD: http://bit.ly/1EyV2Qu

Current cost: $1.99

A popular sight word recognition and practice game.

Sight Word Ninja: http://bit.ly/1Ag8reZ

Current cost: Free

A popular sight word recognition and practice game for young children.

 ## Online Reading Resources

To learn more about the use of sight words during reading, explore these online resources:

- Logsdon, A. (n.d.). *Sight word lists–Teach your child early sight words to improve reading.* (A short article that provides links to various resources and describes sight word use during reading.)

  Retrieved from http://abt.cm/14GguDU

- Unknown Author. (n.d.). Teaching sight words: Effective strategies for reading success. *K12 Reader.* (Online journal). (An article on the role of sight word knowledge during reading and how to support this in your classroom.)

  Retrieved from http://www.k12reader.com/sight-word-teaching-strategies/

- Unknown Author. (n.d.) *Dolch Sight Word List.* The Dolch list organized by grade level (1–3).

  Retrieved from http://www.mrsperkins.com/dolch-words-all-alpha.html (Includes a printable version of the Dolch Word List.)

7

Morphemic Analysis

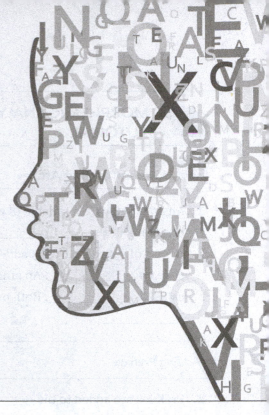

 ## INTRODUCTION

A *morpheme* is the smallest unit of meaning in a word. Some morphemes can stand alone as a meaning-bearing unit. For example, the word *cat* contains a single morpheme and can stand alone. Such morphemes are called free morphemes. Other morphemes are meaning bearing but cannot stand alone. For example, the s̲ in *cats* has meaning, indicating that there is more than one cat, but the s̲ cannot stand alone without *cat*. Morphemes such as the s̲ in *cats̲* are called bound morphemes.

Morphemic analysis involves looking at word parts, such as prefixes, suffixes, and root words, to help determine a word's meaning. The content of morphemic analysis in reading instruction is the study of *affixes* (i.e., both prefixes and suffixes), root words, and compound words. Morphemic analysis is often used with English Learners or struggling readers to help them build vocabulary, and the strategies presented in this book help all learners pronounce the word parts associated with morphemic analysis.

MORPHEMIC ANALYSIS: AN INTERACTIVE TUTORIAL

Understanding Affixes

1. An *affix* refers to a syllable or a letter combination added to the beginning or the _____ of a word to change its meaning or part of speech. An affix added to the beginning of a word is called a _____. An affix added to the end of a word is called a _____. Both prefixes and suffixes are called _____.	end prefix suffix affixes

Adding Prefixes

2. Prefixes are added to the _____ of words to change their meaning. Add the prefix to the base (or root) words below: <u>un</u> to the base *happy* _____ <u>dis</u> to the base *regard* _____ <u>en</u> to the base *able* _____ <u>ex</u> to the base *change* _____	beginnings *unhappy* *disregard* *enable* *exchange*
3. Notice that the spelling of the root word was _____ changed when the prefix was added, but the _____ of the base word changed.	not meaning

Prefix Generalization

4. When added to a base word, a prefix changes the _____ but not the _____ of the base word.	meaning spelling
5. You can tell the meaning of a prefix by noticing how it changes the meaning of the root word to which it is added. The word *unhappy* differs from *happy* in that the _____ <u>un</u> has been added to happy.	prefix
6. *Happy* means glad, but *unhappy* means _____ glad. The prefix <u>un</u> means _____.	not not

7. From the following list of words, identify the prefix and indicate its meaning.

	Prefix	*Meaning*
dislike	_____	_____
enable	_____	_____
inconsistent	_____	_____
unseen	_____	_____
retake	_____	_____
preview	_____	_____

dis, not
en, make
in, not
un, not
re, again
pre, before

The meaning of a _____ can be determined by the manner in which it _____ the meaning of the base word.

prefix
changes (alters)

Adding Suffixes

8. Suffixes are additions to the _____ of root words and can alter both a word's grammatical function (part of speech) and/or its meaning. There are two important types of suffixes. One type of suffix is called an *inflectional ending* or an *inflection*. Another type of suffix is a *derivational suffix*.

ends

9. An inflectional ending often changes the grammatical function but not the core meaning of the root word to which it is added. Common _____ endings are s, es(s), ing, ed, er, est, and ly.

inflectional

Notice how the inflectional endings in the following words do not alter the root word's central meaning:

cat	*cats* singular changed to _____	plural
host	*hostess* masculine changed to _____	feminine
lean	*leaner* adjective changed to _____	comparative
happy	*happily* adjective changed to _____	adverb

10. Apostrophes followed by s also are categorized as inflectional _____. For example, the meaning of *cat* when followed by 's indicates _____.

endings
possession

11. You probably noticed that the inflectional endings that you added produced variations but did not change the root word's basic _____. For example, adding the _____ suffix <u>s</u> to the root word *cat* doesn't change the basic meaning of the root word (the inflectional suffix <u>s</u> just changed the meaning to more than one cat).	meaning, inflectional
12. In contrast, adding derivational suffixes produces a _____ word. For example, adding the suffix <u>ity</u> to the word *dense*, making the word *density*, changes the root word's _____.	new meaning
13. When deciding if an affix is inflectional or derivational, you will need to look at its part of speech and decide whether or not the root word's meaning has _____. Sometimes, the same affix can be derivational with one root word and part of speech but inflectional with other words or parts of speech. An example is the suffix <u>er</u>. Consider the following sentences and <u>er</u> suffix used with *larger* and *cooker* and state when it is being used as an inflectional or a derivational suffix. (a) Her car is larg<u>er</u> than mine. _____ (b) An appliance, such as a slow cook<u>er</u>, can be useful for making stews. _____	changed inflectional derivational

■ **Suffix Generalization 1**

14. Add the inflectional ending <u>ing</u> to these words: *hope* _____ *love* _____ *write* _____ *make* _____	*hoping* *loving* *writing* *making*
15. To add the inflectional ending <u>ing</u>, the final <u>e</u> was _____ from the base word.	dropped (omitted)
16. Complete the following generalization: When adding the inflectional ending _____ to a base word that ends in <u>e</u>, you usually drop the _____ and add the inflectional ending.	ing vowel (<u>e</u>)

17. This generalization also applies to words when inflectional endings that begin with a vowel are added. Apply this generalization by adding the suffix to the following words:

ed to *hope*	_____	*hoped*
er to *write*	_____	*writer*
es to *love*	_____	*loves*
ing to *make*	_____	*making*

18. Complete the following generalization: When adding an inflectional ending that begins with a _____ to a base word that ends in _____, you usually drop the final _____ and add the inflectional ending.

vowel

e

e

■ Suffix Generalization 2

19. Above the last three letters in the following words, mark V over the vowels and C over the consonants, as shown with *hop*.

cvc
hop

_____
occur

_____
sit

_____
skip

What is the pattern that you marked? _____

cvc
occur

cvc
sit

cvc
skip

CVC

20. Add ing to *hop* and *sit*.

_____ _____

Add ed to *occur* and *skip*.

_____ _____

hopping, sitting

occurred, skipped

21. There are three important things to notice in the example shown in item 20:

(a) Do the inflectional endings in item 20 begin with a vowel or consonant? _____

(b) To add the inflectional ending, the final consonant in the root word was _____.

(c) The last three letters of the base words have a _____ pattern.

vowel

doubled

CVC

22. Based on what you noticed in item 20, complete the following generalization: When adding an inflectional ending that begins with a vowel to a base word that has a _____ pattern for its last three letters, the last consonant of the root word is usually _____.	CVC doubled

Suffix Generalization 3

23. To determine this generalization, state what you notice in the following example: Add ing to *sleep* _____ ed to *wash* _____ er to *short* _____ en to *eat* _____	*sleeping* *washed* *shorter* *eaten*
24. Do the root words in item 23 end in a vowel or a consonant? _____	consonant
25. Do any of the base words in item 23 end in the pattern CVC? _____	no
26. What do you notice about the inflectional endings in item 23? These inflectional endings begin with a _____.	vowel
27. Is either the base word or the suffix changed when they are joined? _____	no
28. Based on your observations about the examples in item 23, complete the following generalization: When you add an inflectional ending that begins with a vowel to a base word that ends in a consonant but not in the pattern of _____, neither the _____ nor the inflectional ending is changed.	CVC base

29. Note the pattern of the last two letters of the following words:

try   candy   cry   fly

The last letter in each word is _____, which is preceded
by a _____.

y
consonant

30. Add the inflectional endings to the following words:

<u>ed</u> to *try*   _____

<u>es</u> to *candy*   _____

<u>ed</u> to *cry*   _____

<u>es</u> to *fly*   _____

tried
candies
cried
flies

31. The last letter in each of the above base words was

_____ and was changed to _____ before the
inflectional ending was added. The inflectional endings in item 30
begin with the letter _____.

y, i
e

32. Complete the following generalization: When you add an

inflectional ending that begins with _____ to a base word

that ends in a consonant plus _____ pattern, you usually

change the <u>y</u> to _____ and add the inflectional ending.

e
y
i

✓ **SELF-CHECK FOR CHAPTER 7**

1. Add the inflectional endings to the items below.

<u>ed</u> to *bless*   _____

<u>ing</u> to *drive*   _____

<u>er</u> to *boast*   _____

<u>est</u> to *lazy*   _____

blessed
driving
boaster
laziest

2. If readers look at *sloping* and do not know it on sight, they might

try to take off the _____ and examine the root word.

After taking off the <u>ing</u> suffix, _____ would be left.

Note the structure of what is left after the <u>ing</u> suffix is removed. It

apparently ends in what type of letter pattern? _____

Was the final consonant doubled when the <u>ing</u> was added?

_____

suffix (ing)
slop
<u>CVC</u>
no

Given that the final consonant was not doubled, would you say that *slop* is the root word? _____	no
Slop is not the root word because the final consonant was not _____ when the suffix was added.	doubled
The base word for *sloping* is, therefore, probably _____.	*slope*
Note that this visual clue guides the reader to the pronunciation of the word because the final <u>e</u> determines the _____ of the first vowel.	sound
A reader would have to imagine the base word to be _____ with the inflectional ending _____ added.	*slope*, <u>ing</u>

3. Write the base word for the following words:

sloping	_____	*slope*
tempting	_____	*temp*
slopping	_____	*slop*
dozing	_____	*doze*
given	_____	*give*

PRACTICAL EXAMPLES AND RESOURCES FOR TEACHING MORPHEMIC ANALYSIS IN YOUR CLASSROOM

Take a Look Videos

Take a look at this video from the classroom: https://www.youtube.com/watch?v=Ru73bf51uu4.

It shows a classroom example of a teacher teaching prefixes and suffixes.

Take a look at this video from another classroom: https://www.youtube.com/watch?v=Qt5W2wgIqsk.

The teacher shows how to make a simple prefix word game. This activity can be used for review by children independently or, together with a teacher, for initial teaching.

Take a look at this video: https://www.youtube.com/watch?v=CBij9-WFLTc.

It shows how to make and use "Flip-it" word cards. The video presents the activity as a vocabulary building exercise, but it can also be used as a word attack activity.

Take a look at this video from the classroom: https://www.youtube.com/watch?v=GODT3SFDR70.

The teacher conducts a review of prefixes and begins to introduce suffixes.

 Lesson Suggestions

Flip-a-Chip: Examining Affixes and Roots to Build Vocabulary (http://bit.ly/1DKAelV).
This *ReadWriteThink* lesson shows students how different affixes and roots can be joined to make words and then placed into a context-rich paragraph.

Rooting Out Meaning: Morpheme Match-Ups in the Primary Grades (http://bit.ly/14gYfnO).
A *ReadWriteThink* lesson that encourages students to use morphemes to deconstruct and construct words.

Improve Comprehension: A Word Game Using Root Words and Affixes (http://bit.ly/1ACfuvD).
A *ReadWriteThink* lesson where students learn root words and affixes in a variety of ways using a list of about 20 common but challenging words.

 Apps for Classroom Use

Bluster!: http://bit.ly/1srIyVI
   Current cost: Free

   A set of games, at different levels, that can be related to various areas of word attack; it includes prefix and suffix games.

Syllable Blastoff: http://bit.ly/1679BMm
   Current cost: $9.99

   Prompts educators through a succession of prefixes, stem words, and prefixes with their students. Can be used to provide automated flash cards or as a tool to track student's progress. Can be customized to include segments individually or to combine two or three segments.

Online Reading Resources

To learn more about the use of morphemic analysis during reading, explore these online resources:

- Baumann, J., Edwards, E. C., Font, G., Tereshinski, C. A., Kame'enui, E. J., & Olejnik, S. (2002). Teaching morphemic and contextual analysis to fifth-grade students. *Reading Research Quarterly*, *37*, 150–176. (A study of instruction in morphemic and contextual analysis among fifth grade readers.)

  Retrieved from http://128.220.219.39/olms/data/resource/2041/la_vocab _research.pdf

- Mountain, L. (2005). ROOTing out meaning: More morphemic analysis for primary pupils. *Reading Teacher*, *58*, 742–749. (This article explains how teachers integrated morphemic analysis instruction to help students learn about suffixes, prefixes, and root words.)

8

Chunking Words into Smaller Units: Syllabication and Structural Analysis

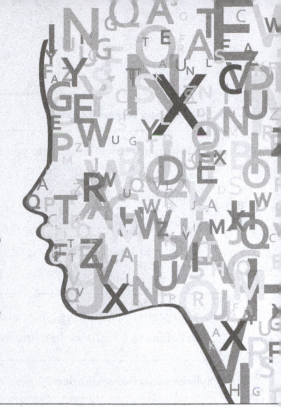

INTRODUCTION

Breaking words into smaller units can help readers determine a word's pronunciation and meaning. Often, teachers refer to this as *chunking* a word. Chunking is part of structural analysis, and some curriculum materials refer to it as syllabication.

Recognizing syllable units within words is a word analysis strategy that falls under the heading of structural analysis. Syllables usually do not have meaning in themselves, but by chunking words into their smaller parts, readers are often able to pronounce the parts and blend them into familiar words. Although some syllabication generalizations are important for teachers and students to know, others are inconsistent in their application and may be of little value. We discuss the most consistent and useful syllable generalizations in this chapter.

SYLLABICATION AND STRUCTURAL ANALYSIS: AN INTERACTIVE TUTORIAL

Syllabication

1. Recognizing syllable units within words is a word analysis strategy that falls under the heading of structural analysis. Often, syllables are taught as visual clues, as well as _____ clues.

   pronunciation

2. How many vowel sounds do you hear in the following words?
 	
   cat _____   *apple* _____
 	
   happiness _____   *rate* _____
 	
   philosophy _____   *tiger* _____
 	
Is the number of syllables equal to the number of vowel sounds?
 	
_____
	one, two
	
	three, one
	
	four, two
	
	yes

3. Complete the following generalization: There are as many syllables in a word as there are vowel _____.	sounds (phonemes)

■ **Syllabication Generalization 2**

4. How many vowel sounds do you hear in the following words?
 	
   hope _____   *love* _____
 	
   write _____   *hate* _____
 	
Each of the above words has _____ vowels and _____ vowel sound. The final _____ is silent.
	one, one
	
	one, one
	
	two
	one, vowel (e)

5. How many vowel sounds do you hear in the following words?
 	
   read _____   *feed* _____
 	
   rain _____   *coat* _____
 	
How many vowels are in these words? _____ The second _____ in these words is _____ (a pattern marker).
	one, one
	
	one, one
	
	two
	vowel, silent

6. Complete the following generalization: There are two situations when a vowel letter usually does not represent a sound. When these structures appear, there are _____ vowels but only one vowel _____; thus, the two vowels are in one syllable.	two sound
7. These first two generalizations relate directly to knowledge that children should have prior to learning the remaining generalizations. As such, they are not, strictly speaking, generalizations applied to _____ but refer, instead, to visual and sound clues that are helpful when chunking words.	syllabication

Chunking Words into Smaller Units   86

8. Place a V over the first and last vowels and a C over the consonants that are between the vowels in the following words, as shown in this example:

   VCCV
   Example: picnic

   _____   _____
   pencil   *index*

   _____
   window

   The words are similar because they contain the _____ pattern.

VCCV *pencil*	VCCV *index*
VCCV *window*	
VCCV	

9. Divide the following words into syllables:

   VCCV
   Example: pic/nic

   _____   _____
   pencil   *index*

   _____
   window

VC CV *pen/cil*	VC CV *in/dex*
VC CV *win/dow*	

10. What do you notice about where you divided the words in items 8 and 9? You divided the words _____ the consonants.

    between

11. Complete the following generalization: When a word has the pattern VCCV, you usually divide the word _____ the _____.

    between

    consonants

12. Double consonants in the VCCV pattern signal possible exceptions to the VCCV generalization. For example, the words *ladder, dagger, letter,* and *butter* fit the VCCV pattern. If these words were divided between the two identical consonants as *lad/der, dag/ger, let/ter,* and *but/ter*, there might be the tendency to produce two phonemes for the double letter. If the words were divided into _____ as *ladd/er, dagg/er, lett/er,* and *butt/er*, only one phoneme would be associated with the double letter. There is a variance in how dictionaries divide such words into syllables.

    syllables

13. However, words such as *midday* and *overrate* do follow the VCCV generalization as both of the middle consonants are _____ because these words are _____ words.	pronounced, compound

■ **Syllabication Generalization 4 (V/CV or VC/V)**

14. Divide the following words into syllables: begin _____ acorn _____ pupil _____ over _____	be/gin, a/corn pu/pil, o/ver
15. Mark the vowels and consonants starting with the first vowel and going to the last, as shown with *begin*. Example: begin (vcv) _____ acorn _____ pupil _____ over	vcv acorn vcv over vcv pupil
16. The words in item 15 have a similar structure. Each word contains the VCV pattern, and you divided the words _____ the first vowel.	after
17. Complete the following generalization: When a word has the structure _____, you usually divide the word after the _____ vowel. This generalization has two common exceptions, which are presented next.	VCV first
18. Many words with a vowel followed by a single consonant are divided into syllables after, instead of _____ the consonant. Pronounce the following words and then divide them into syllables: robin _____ rivet _____ limit _____ lemon _____ magic _____ rapid _____ In these words, the consonant following the first vowel is part of the _____ syllable.	before rob/in, riv/et lim/it, lem/on mag/ic, rap/id first

19. The words *robot* and *robin* both have the _____ structure. In *robot* the first syllable ends with the vowel; in *robin*, the first syllable ends with the _____.	VCV consonant
20. If you are trying to determine the pronunciation of an unfamiliar word with the <u>VCV</u> structure, remember that the word might be divided into syllables after the first vowel, as in *robot*, or after the vowel and the _____, as in *robin*.	consonant
21. The second exception to the VCV generalization can be inferred from the following example. Divide these words into syllables: forest _____ chorus _____ miracle _____ sterile _____	for/est, chor/us mir/a/cle, ster/ile
22. Although the fourth syllabication generalization states that the CVC pattern means that words are usually divided _____ the consonant, this did not apply in the previous example.	before
23. Look back at how you divided the words in item 21. What consonant follows the first vowel? _____	r
24. Thus, when dividing words according to the fourth syllabication generalization, the following must also be considered: When the structure _____ appears in a word and the consonant is an <u>r</u>, there can be an exception to the fourth syllabication generalization, and the _____ may go with the preceding vowel in the syllable.	VCV r

▪ **Syllabication Generalization 5 (<u>V/digraph V</u> or <u>V/blend V</u>)**

25. Divide the following words into syllables: author _____ either _____ vibrate _____ emblem _____	au/thor, ei/ther vi/brate, em/blem
26. The two consonants after the syllable division in these words are either blends or _____ and are _____ divided for syllabication.	digraphs, not

27. Complete the following generalization: When dividing words into syllables, consonant blends and _____ are generally not _____. (*Note:* This can be applied regardless of other structures present, such as <u>VCCV</u> or <u>VCV</u>.)	digraphs divided

■ Syllabication Generalization 6 (Compound Words)

28. Compound words are formed when two words are joined to form a new word. *Birthday, cannot, baseball,* and *drugstore* are all _____ words.	compound
29. Divide the following words into syllables: *birthday* _____ *cannot* _____ *baseball* _____ *drugstore* _____ Did you notice that each _____ is a complete word?	*birth/day, can/not* *base/ball, drug/store* syllable
30. Complete the following generalization: When dividing _____ words into syllables, each word is a separate _____, or morpheme.	compound syllable

■ Syllabication Generalization 7

31. Divide the following words into syllables: *goodness* _____ *unlock* _____ *regardless* _____ *nonsense* _____	*good/ness, un/lock* *re/gard/less, non/sense*
32. Each word contains prefixes or suffixes, which are also called _____.	affixes
33. Are the prefixes and suffixes separate syllables? _____	yes
34. Complete the following generalization: Prefixes and suffixes are usually separate _____.	syllables

■ Syllabication Generalization 8 (<u>V</u>/<u>C</u> + <u>le</u>)

35. The words *ankle, simple, startle, needle* end with the letters _____.	<u>le</u>

36. Divide these words into syllables: ankle _____ simple _____ startle _____ needle _____	*an/kle, sim/ple* *star/tle, nee/dle*
37. What type of letter appears before the <u>le</u>? _____	consonant
38. Look back at the way you divided the words in item 36. The final syllable is composed of the consonant plus the _____.	<u>le</u>
39. Complete the following generalization: In a word that ends in le preceded by a _____, the last syllable usually begins with the consonant preceding the _____. This generalization has fairly high utility because most exceptions involve the suffix <u>able</u>.	consonant <u>le</u>

USING SYLLABICATION TO HELP WITH PRONUNCIATION

40. One purpose for dividing words into syllables is to arrive at smaller pronunciation units. Determining the appropriate _____ sounds within syllables can aid in _____, which helps in decoding a word. Pronunciation generalizations are based on the appropriate division of words into syllables and the identification of the vowel _____ in each syllable.	vowel, pronunciation sound
41. As you work toward the pronunciation of an unfamiliar word, you will often come close to its _____ yet not produce the exact, "correct" pronunciation. However, approximations of the correct pronunciation can be very useful if the word is part of your oral vocabulary because other clues will act _____ with the approximation to help you determine the correct pronunciation of the word.	pronunciation together
42. Before reading the pronunciation generalizations, below, here are two useful definitions to keep in mind: (a) *Closed syllables* are _____ that contain one vowel and end in a consonant, such as *sun* or *sig/nal*. (b) *Open syllables* are syllables that end in a vowel, such as *me* or *be/gin*.	syllables

Pronunciation Generalization 1

43. What kind of letter do the words *get, pin, ran, sun, rot* end with? _____	consonant
44. In the words *get, pin, ran, sun, rot* does the vowel sound long (glided) or short (unglided)? _____	short (unglided)
45. Recall that syllables containing one vowel and ending with a consonant are called _____ syllables.	closed
46. Complete the following generalization: Closed syllables usually contain _____, or unglided, vowel sounds. This generalization also applies to syllables in words of more than one syllable, for example, *picnic (pic/nic), signal (sig/nal).*	short

Pronunciation Generalization 2

47. What is the sound of the vowel in the words *high, night, kind, find, cold, told*? _____	long (glided)
48. Are the words in item 47 closed syllables? _____	yes
49. Write the vowel and the two letters that follow it: *high, night* _____ *find, kind* _____ *cold, told* _____ These are letter structures that call for long vowel sounds in _____ syllables.	igh ind old closed
50. Complete the following generalization: When the structures <u>igh</u>, <u>old</u>, and _____ appear in a word, the vowel sound is usually _____, even though the syllable is closed.	ind long (glided)

Pronunciation Generalization 3

51. In the following words, are the underlined syllables closed? _____ *for/est thir/sty pur/suit car/toon* What letter follows the first vowel in each word? _____	yes r
52. Is the first vowel in the underlined syllables in item 51 long or short? _____	neither (it is r-controlled)
53. Complete the following generalization: The consonant _____ following a vowel usually creates a closed syllable but may result in an _____ vowel sound. This can be viewed as an exception to the first pronunciation generalization.	r r-controlled

Pronunciation Generalization 4

54. The last letter in the words *be, go, me* is a _____.	vowel
55. Are the vowel sounds in the words *be, go, me* long (glided) or short (unglided)? _____	long (glided)
56. Recall that _____ syllables occur when a vowel is the last letter in the _____. This generalization applies to syllables in words of more than one syllable, for example, *o/pen, be/gin, la/zy, pu/pil.*	open syllable
57. Complete the following generalization: Open syllables usually end with _____ vowel sounds.	long (glided)

Pronunciation Generalization 5

58. Recall that two vowels appearing side by side usually represent _____ vowel sound, as seen in the words: *pain, read, pail, seek.*	one

59. This generalization also applies to words of more than one syllable. Pronounce the following words: *teacher* *obtain* *detail* *moaning* How many vowels are there in these words? _____ How many vowel sounds? _____	three two
60. Complete the following generalization: Two vowels together usually indicate that the first one is long and the second one is _____, unless the vowel combination is a vowel diphthong or a variant vowel _____.	silent digraph

Pronunciation Generalization 6

61. Recall that a final <u>e</u> preceded by a single consonant usually indicates that the preceding vowel is _____, with the <u>e</u> itself being _____ (or a marker). Thus, the pattern of the following words calls for _____ vowel sound.
 	
      ate   *cake*   *hope*   *kite*
 	
This generalization also _____ to words of more than one syllable. Pronounce the following words (noticing the last syllable):
 	
      imi<u>tate</u>   *grap<u>hite</u>*   *tele<u>scope</u>*   *a<u>wake</u>*
	long
	silent
	one
	
	applies

62. Complete the following generalization: When a word ends in <u>e</u> preceded by a single consonant, the vowel before the consonant is usually _____.	long
63. Pronounce the following words. Notice that they all end in e. *fence* *dance* *sledge* Is the first vowel long or short? _____ How many consonants are between the first vowel and the final <u>e</u>? _____ When a word ends in <u>e</u> but is not preceded by a single consonant, the final <u>e</u> may be silent but does not affect the preceding _____ sound.	 short two vowel

1. *Divide Words Number of Syllables* (The word *silent* shows an example.)

silent	si/lent	two	
helmet	_____	_____	hel/met, two
demon	_____	_____	de/mon, two
Arab	_____	_____	Ar/ab, two
bismuth	_____	_____	bis/muth, two
arable	_____	_____	ar/a/ble, three
lentil	_____	_____	len/til, two

2. What is the visual clue to each syllable division; that is, what pattern can you see?

Example: silent	VCV	
helmet	_____	VCCV
demon	_____	VCV
Arab	_____	VrV
bismuth	_____	VCCV
arable	_____	VrV, ble
lentil	_____	VCCV

3. Indicate each vowel sound in the following words:

Example: sup	short u	
find	_____	long i
soften	_____	short o, short e
gain	_____	long a
journey	_____	r-controlled u, short e
sparkle	_____	r-controlled a
dance	_____	short a
token	_____	long o, short e

PRACTICAL EXAMPLES AND RESOURCES FOR TEACHING CHUNKING SKILLS IN YOUR CLASSROOM

 ## Take a Look Videos

Take a look at this teacher in the classroom: https://www.youtube.com/watch?v=G8kzelDZGDo.

An example of a kindergarten teacher using a clapping technique to teach the concept of syllables.

 ## Lesson Suggestions

Teaching Syllable Segmentation (http://bit.ly/16byYgX).

This lesson provides several activities to help young children realize that words are composed of syllables.

Teaching Syllables (http://bit.ly/1yYCVA0).

A Pinterest "board" containing activities and suggestions from teachers and others about teaching syllables, many with examples.

 ## Apps for Classroom Use

Syllables: http://bit.ly/1Lw4TbQ

 Current cost; $0.99

  Targets syllabication and accent/pronunciation emphasis, and can be helpful as a syllabication exercise and pronunciation guide for English Learners.

Syllable Splash: http://bit.ly/1vlKMIO

 Current cost: $7.99

  Aims to teach syllable segmentation through a multiplayer activity, using images and words from one to four syllables.

Syllable Word Search: http://bit.ly/1yTEDxY

 Current cost: Free

  A "memory card + word search" style game that can provide practice in finding syllables and blending them into words.

To learn more about the use of chunking words into smaller units during reading, explore these online resources:

- Knight-McKenna, M. (2008). Syllable types: A strategy for reading multisyllabic words. *Teaching Exceptional Children.* (An article that shows how to teach struggling readers how to use chunking and syllabication strategies to recognize multisyllabic words.)
  Retrieved from http://bit.ly/1zlowOU

- Pacheco, M. B., & Goodwin, A. P. (2013). Putting two and two together: Middle school students' morphological problem-solving strategies for unknown words. *Journal of Adolescent & Adult Literacy, 56*(7), 541–553. (An article discussing root words and affixes, as well as various teaching strategies and recommendations appropriate for middle school children.)
  Retrieved from http://bit.ly/1EWvPge

9

The Dictionary and Word Analysis

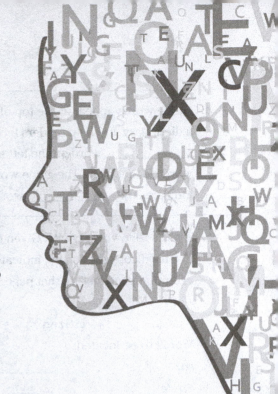

INTRODUCTION

Except in lower grade levels where picture dictionaries are still used and can be helpful for teaching alphabetizing and pronunciation, online dictionaries, as well as dictionaries and spelling checkers built into word processing software, are increasingly used to confirm spelling or to find word meanings. However, whether in digital or printed form, dictionaries can serve as a reference for confirming and studying pronunciations of words. In this chapter, we limit our discussion to using a dictionary to support word analysis, especially for children in the early grades.

THE DICTIONARY AND WORD ANALYSIS: AN INTERACTIVE TUTORIAL

Locating Words in a Dictionary

1. Whether online or in traditional form, a dictionary can be a helpful word analysis tool. Usually, however, dictionaries are used only when pronunciation generalizations, structural _____, and context clues are not effective.	analysis
2. To use a dictionary, a child must know how to alphabetize by at least the _____ letter of a word and must be able to use _____ to select one meaning from alternatives.	first context

3. Guide words appear at the top of each page in the body of a dictionary and help readers locate particular words. The _____ word on the left side of the page indicates the first word on that page. The guide word on the right side of the page indicates the _____ word on that page.	guide last
4. Try the following activity. Given the set of boldface guide words in a hard copy dictionary, indicate whether the word to be located is on that page, before that page, or after that page. **citizen** • **clamp** Words to be located: *car* _____ *circle* _____ *clam* _____ *city* _____ *clap* _____	 before before on on after
5. Online dictionaries, dictionaries used within word processing software, as well as traditional dictionaries provide several types of information. They specify pronunciation, parts of speech, syllabication, and a word's _____.	meaning(s)

Using a Dictionary to Help Determine Pronunciation

6. Regardless of the dictionary used, the _____ key follows the main entry word. For example, if the entry word is *mimic*, you would see
 	
    mim·ic (mim´ik) *n.*
    The "*n.*" following the pronunciation entry indicates a word's part of speech. In this case, *mimic* is defined as a _____. Sometimes, the part of speech is written out completely, as in "noun" or "verb."
	pronunciation
	
	noun

7. The information provided for a main entry word includes how to pronounce the entry word, how it should be divided into _____, which syllable should be accented, and the word's part of _____.	 syllables speech

8. Dictionaries use diacritical marks and keywords to indicate pronunciation. In addition, online and digital dictionaries often allow users to click on the word and hear it pronounced. __________ marks indicate stress or accents of syllables within words and show vowel __________ as being either long (glided) or short (unglided). The common diacritical marks are as follows: ´ indicates stress or accent – appears above a vowel and indicates a long vowel sound ˘ appears above a vowel and indicates a short vowel sound	Diacritical pronunciations
9. Sometimes, a dictionary entry will contain more than one accent mark, with one accent mark showing darker than the other(s). The syllable before the __________ accent mark gets more __________. This can be especially helpful to young children and English Learners, because some words are spelled the same way but are pronounced differently. Sometimes, the differences in the pronunciation of words is related to which syllable is __________.	darker emphasis accented (emphasized)
10. At times, a word might have more than one acceptable pronunciation. For example, *data* can be pronounced two different ways, with the first vowel being either __________ or long. If there is more than one pronunciation shown in the dictionary entry, both are acceptable, but the one shown __________ is preferred.	short first

Using a Dictionary to Help Determine Meaning

11. In addition to __________, dictionaries also help a reader determine a word's meaning by providing common definitions for each entry word. __________ usually appear after the word's part of speech is given, for example, after the word has been designated as a noun, a verb, an adjective, or an adverb.	pronunciation Definitions
12. For words with only one definition, using a dictionary to help a reader determine meaning is quite simple. Many words, however, have two or more __________. Even online dictionaries and common word processing software such as Microsoft's Word®	definitions

(www://products.office.com/en-us/word), or LibreOffice (http://www.libreoffice.org), show several meanings for almost every word.	
13. For example, the word *conductor* is usually shown as having at least three main _____: a leader or director, as in an orchestra or choir conductor; someone who collects fares, as in a train or streetcar conductor; or something that conveys heat or electricity, as in an electrical conductor. When there is more than one definition, readers must _____ one of the definitions and the original _____ in which the word occurred.	entries (definitions) match context
14. Definitions are usually placed in order from the most common meaning to the least common meaning. Beginning readers often need to be taught that it is not appropriate to use the first _____ that appears without checking the _____ in which the word is used.	definition context

☑ SELF-CHECK FOR CHAPTER 9

1. If the guide words are **island** and **isolate**, would the following words appear on that page, before that page, or on after that page? *isobar* _____ *irritable* _____ *isthmus* _____ *isoglass* _____ *island* _____ *isoprene* _____	 on before after on on after
2. Look at the entry **mon·ey** (mŭn´e) *n.* What part of speech is it? _____ How would you pronounce <u>ey</u>? _____ Which syllable is accented? _____	 noun long <u>e</u> first
3. Look at the entry **lac·tose** (lak´tos) *n.* What is the vowel sound for the <u>o</u> in lactose? _____ What is the consonant sound for the <u>c</u>? _____ Which syllable is accented? _____	 long <u>o</u> hard <u>c</u> (or <u>k</u>) first

4. When an entry has multiple meanings listed, readers must check the _____ where they encountered the word to determine the appropriate _____.

context

meaning (or definition)

PRACTICAL EXAMPLES AND RESOURCES FOR TEACHING DICTIONARY SKILLS IN YOUR CLASSROOM

Many useful online dictionaries are available at no cost. A list of online dictionary resources can be found at http://www.onelook.com, http://www.yourdictionary.com, and http://bit.ly/1Ds3TQw. Also, simply entering "what does <a given word> mean" in a search engine will usually provide a word's meaning(s) and pronunciation information, or links to resources that will do so. With many search engines you can just enter the following into the keyword window: define: <your desired word> and the word's definition and pronunciation key will appear without requiring a link to a dictionary site.

While paper-based dictionaries are popular and appropriate for primary-grade children, many online picture dictionaries are available as well. Although picture dictionaries are often organized by category (animals, clothing, colors, and so on), and not all provide pronunciation guides, many online dictionaries pronounce the word when the picture or word is clicked. This is often beneficial for young children or English Learners (see, for example, www.opdome.com). Online picture and photo dictionaries can be useful for teachers in classrooms with whiteboard or other projection capabilities, tablets, or computers and can be incorporated into lessons on pronunciation and other word attack strategies, including syllabication and affixes.

Take a Look Videos

Take a look at this video, a short demonstration of how the *Dictionary.com* app can be used for pronunciation practice on a mobile device: https://www.youtube.com/watch?v=tOoKyV8wZc0.

As is pointed out, the demonstrated procedure may be especially useful for English Learners.

Lesson Suggestions

My Own Picture Dictionary (http://bit.ly/1Cne7EK). Provides suggestions, activities, and instructions for teachers to help young children create their own picture dictionaries using images of people and things that they know and are important to them.

Dictionary Games (http://bit.ly/1uPI8VN). These games include several suggestions from teachers for using the dictionary to teach alphabetizing and find appropriate definitions, plus other dictionary-related activities.

Using Dictionaries (http://bit.ly/1zshpmf). This article provides information about dictionaries and activities to use with students to build knowledge of dictionary layout search and pronunciation keys.

Apps for Classroom Use

Pic Collage: http://bit.ly/1fJ78Y7

 Current cost: Free

  Builds collages using images, videos, and text that can be used to create a classroom picture dictionary. See *Creating a Visual Dictionary on the iPad* (http://bit.ly/1EyudvL) to read a short article that gives a step-by-step procedure that is useful in combination with the *Pic Collage* app

Dictionary.com: http://bit.ly/1d4r302.

 Current cost: Free. The $3.99 paid version deletes advertisements. A popular dictionary that can be used offline. Includes word pronunciation.

Online Reading Resources

To learn more about the use of the dictionary to support word recognition, explore these online resources:

- Lewis, L. (2008). All about words: Dictionary activities. *Education World*. (A short article on dictionary use along with links to several activities to use in class.) Retrieved from http://www.educationworld.com/a_lesson/lesson/lesson206.shtml.

- Fraser, C. A. (1999). The Role of Consulting a Dictionary in Reading and Vocabulary Learning. *Canadian Journal of Applied Linguistics, 21*, 73–89. (A review of research on the use of a dictionary with English Language Learners.) Retrieved from http://bit.ly/1KinUyJ

10

Developmental Spelling Patterns: Insights into the Development of Word Analysis Skills

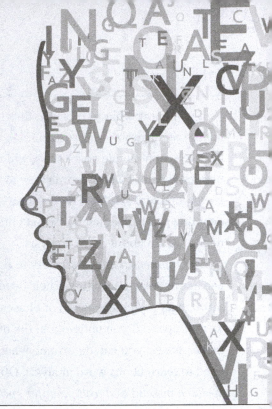

 INTRODUCTION

Look at the following writing sample from a five-year-old child:

I LK MY KTY ("I like my kitty.")

Children tell us what they know about word analysis through the uncorrected spelling patterns they use in their writing. From this sentence, written by a five-year-old child, we can learn many things. Because each word was written separately, we know that this child has developed the ability to hear words as separate entities, which is an important aspect of phonological awareness. Because many of the phonemes are spelled as separate elements, we also know that this child has developed important aspects of phonemic awareness. Notice, too, the correct spelling of the high-frequency sight words "I" and "MY." This indicates that the child is developing sight word knowledge of common words. We also know that this child has not yet developed an understanding of the <u>VCe</u> pattern for long vowels because the word *like* was spelled as "LK." Finally, this child has not yet developed an understanding of the <u>CVC</u> pattern for short vowels because the word *kitty* was spelled "KTY." These last two clues also tell us that this child may not yet be able to identify vowel phonemes in the middle of a word, which is an important aspect of phonemic awareness.

If you know what to look for, developmental spelling is a powerful source of diagnostic information. It can indicate if children have developed phonemic awareness, which phonic patterns they understand, and which words they already know as sight words. Developmental spelling is a "window" to word analysis knowledge, enabling you to see much of what children already know and what they need to learn about word analysis.

Developmental spelling refers to the spelling patterns children use in uncorrected writing. Their developmental spelling progresses through a predictable series of phases until more standard spelling forms appear. If you understand the developmental progression of these phases, you can determine what children know, and what they need to learn about word analysis. Often, people use the term *invented spelling* instead of *developmental spelling* because children appear to invent the spelling rules through their writing activities, gradually inducing standard spelling patterns.

The developmental spelling checklist in Figure 1 will help you to analyze and track the progression of children's word analysis skills through the patterns of their uncorrected writing and spelling. It shows each of the five major phases of developmental spelling, patterns in each phase, and what a student typically knows about word analysis in each phase. This chapter will describe each of the major phases children pass through and explains how each phase indicates something important about their emerging skills with word analysis.

FIGURE 1   The Leu and Kinzer Developmental Spelling Checklist.

Student _____

Teacher _____

School Year _____

A. Precommunicative Phase

	School Quarter

Pattern	What the child knows	I	II	III	IV
1. Random drawing	Tool knowledge				
2. Organized lines	Left to right/There is a system here but what are the rules?				
3. Letter components	Letters are central elements				
4. Random letters	Letter formation				

B. Semiphonetic Phase

	School Quarter

Pattern	What the child knows	I	II	III	IV
1. Some systematic meaning	Letters represent sounds/sounds represent meaning				
2. Sounds of letters are names of letters	Letter names are letter sounds				
3. Consonants and long vowels, few short vowels	Consonants carry most information				
4. Spaces between words	What a written word is				

C. Phonetic Phase

	School Quarter

Pattern	What the child knows	I	II	III	IV
1. Most sounds represented in writing	Recognizes most phonological segments				
2. Phonic strategies are used	English is phonetic				

D. Transitional Phase

	School Quarter

Pattern	What the child knows	I	II	III	IV
1. Some irregular, high-frequency sight words spelled correctly	English is not phonetic				

E. Standard Phase

	School Quarter

Pattern	What the child knows	I	II	III	IV
1. Most words spelled correctly	English is and is not phonetic				

2. Misspellings follow these patterns:

_____

_____

_____

_____

Source: Leu, Donald J., & Charles K. Kinzer. *Effective Literacy Instruction K–8: Implementing Best Practice*, 5th ed., © 2003, p. 124. Reprinted and Electronically reproduced by permission of Pearson Education, Inc., New York, NY.

DEVELOPMENTAL SPELLING PATTERNS:
AN INTERACTIVE TUTORIAL

The Precommunicative Phase

1. Children usually begin their writing in a precommunicative phase (see Figure 2). During this phase, writing is characterized by not having a consistent communicative intent. If you ask children what their writing says, they will not understand your question or will create a new _____ each time you ask. Their scribbles indicate that they are developing an understanding of the tools of writing: how to hold a pencil or crayon, how to use it to make marks, and so on.	meaning

FIGURE 2   An Example of a Child's Writing from the Precommunicative Phase.

2. Writing during the early precommunicative phase usually indicates that children have not yet developed phonological or phonemic _____. We do not yet see evidence of written words or letters representing words or sounds. Thus, it is likely that they may be unable to distinguish words, syllables, or sounds as separate units.	awareness
3. As the precommunicative phase progresses, organized lines of scribbles begin to emerge. In the English writing system, lines of scribble usually begin to flow from left to _____, indicating that children have discovered this important principle in our writing system.	right
4. Still later, you may find common letter components appearing, such as circles, vertical lines, horizontal lines, and diagonal lines. Random letters will also appear, but children will be able to tell you only the	

names of these letters, not what their message _____. These features indicate that children are paying attention to letter forms in our writing system but have not yet discovered the alphabetic _____, or the insight that letters represent sounds.	means principle
5. The precommunicative phase is an important one for children. In this phase, they are forming the foundation for important steps, that is, the development of phonemic and phonological _____ and the discovery of the alphabetic _____.	awareness principle

The Semiphonetic Phase

6. Next, children usually enter a semiphonetic phase (see Figure 3). Children discover that letters represent sounds in oral language. Developing an understanding of this _____ principle is an important step. It happens in conjunction with the development of phonological and _____ awareness. Both of these developments help children discover that writing is used to communicate meaning.	alphabetic phonemic

FIGURE 3 An Example of a Child's Writing from the Semiphonetic Phase. ("I Read the Book.")

7. During the semiphonetic _____, children often believe that the names of the letters are the sounds that they represent. Thus, messages like *IM5 (I am five.)* may sometimes appear.	phase
8. Most words are at least partially represented in written messages during the semiphonetic phase. This suggests that children have developed _____ awareness because they can identify individual words.	phonological

9. Also, during this time, onset and final consonants appear much more frequently than medial _____, as in these writing samples:
 	
    I WT PZ DR (I want pizza for dinner.)
    SL T KN (The squirrel took the corn.)
 	
This may suggest that a child is able to hear the initial and final phonemes in a word or syllable more easily than a phoneme in the _____ of a word.
	vowels
	
	middle

10. Long vowel sounds are often represented in this phase, far more often than short vowels:
 	
    KN U C BZ (Can you see the birds?)
    I LK BB SR (I like my baby sister.)
 	
This may suggest that a child finds it easier to hear individual long vowel phonemes than short vowel _____. It may also be due to the fact that letter names for vowels are identical to long vowel _____.
	phonemes
	
	sounds

11. Often, children will begin to demonstrate knowledge of high-frequency sight words or words that are very important to them early in their writing. They demonstrate this by correctly spelling common _____ words such as *my, mom, me,* or *I*:
 	
    ME N MOM R SK (Me and my mom were sick.)
    ILMICAT (I love my cat.)
	sight

12. The _____ phase is an important milestone for children. It shows that they have developed an understanding of the _____ principle. Children in this phase understand that letters represent sounds, even though they are not able to successfully hear all the sounds or represent each sound with a letter. This may suggest that children need to develop additional _____ awareness before moving into the next phase.	semiphonetic alphabetic phonemic

📚 The Phonetic Phase

13. When you see writing that looks as if a child is trying to represent nearly every _____ in each word, it is likely that the child is in the _____ phase. The writing in Figure 4 suggests this.	phoneme phonetic

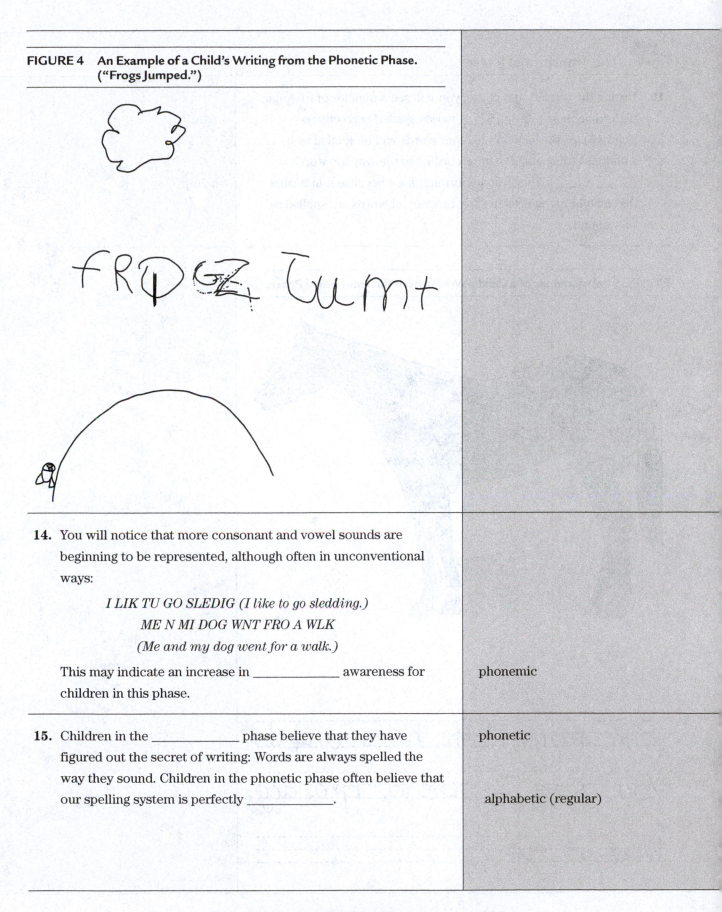

14. You will notice that more consonant and vowel sounds are
beginning to be represented, although often in unconventional
ways:

> *I LIK TU GO SLEDIG (I like to go sledding.)*
> *ME N MI DOG WNT FRO A WLK*
> *(Me and my dog went for a walk.)*

This may indicate an increase in _____ awareness for
children in this phase.   phonemic

15. Children in the _____ phase believe that they have   phonetic
figured out the secret of writing: Words are always spelled the
way they sound. Children in the phonetic phase often believe that
our spelling system is perfectly _____.   alphabetic (regular)

16. During the transitional phase, you will see a number of irregular, high-frequency _____ words spelled correctly (see Figure 5). At the same time, other words will be spelled as if a child is still spelling them according to the way the words _____. This is an important phase because it indicates that a child recognizes the fact that not all words are spelled as they sound.

sight

sound

FIGURE 5   An Example of a Child's Writing from the Transitional Phase.

Brn hors brn hors wut do
You see I see a gra dog
tknr at me

17. During the transitional phase, writing often combines phonic strategies and sight word _____. The sight words that appear most often are very common words (e.g., *and, I, me*) or words that are very important to a child. Notice, for example, the sight words in these sentences:

> *ME AND MY FRNDZ LIK TO PLA*
> *(Me and my friends like to play.)*
> *CAPPY MY DOG WZ HT BY A CAR*
> *(Cappy, my dog, was hit by a car.)*

strategies

The Standard Phase

18. During the _____ phase of developmental spelling, students are able to appropriately combine phonic and _____ word strategies (see Figure 6). For most of us, there will still be some words that are spelled incorrectly. These often are the same set of words or follow a particular pattern. The pattern might include, for example, the misspelling of words with single or double consonants or words that contain certain types of endings. Here is an example:

> *"I liked reading this book because it was*
> *very exciting and it was about the pioneers."*

standard

sight

FIGURE 6   An Example of a Child's Writing from the Standard Phase.

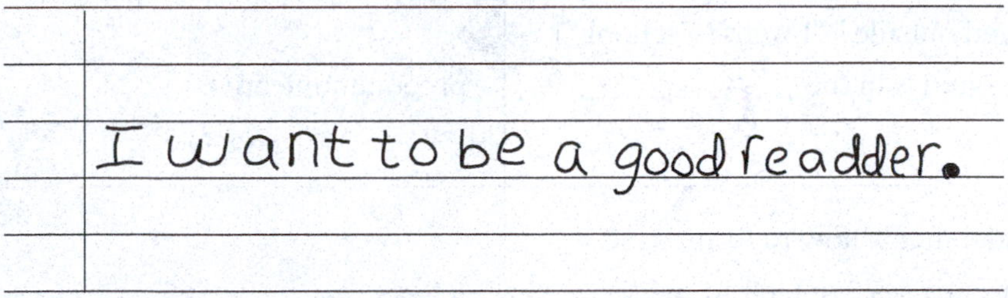

I want to be a good readder.

✓ **SELF-CHECK FOR CHAPTER 10**

Look at this writing from a five-year-old child:
   K P (The cat and the person)

1. We can tell that this child has developed some elements of _____ awareness because each word is represented as separate entities.	phonological
2. This child is probably in the _____ phase of developmental spelling.	semiphonetic
3. The child knows about the _____ progression of print.	left-to-right
4. We also know that this child is beginning to develop an understanding of the _____ principle because two initial consonant sounds are represented by letters.	alphabetic
5. This child has probably not yet developed a complete sense of _____ awareness because not all of the phonemes are represented.	phonemic

Look at this writing from another five-year-old child:
   OEPBEYET (I love my kitty.)

6. Each time this child read the writing, she provided a different meaning ("I love my kitty." "I played outside." "I went to school."). This helps us understand that the child is in the _____ phase of developmental spelling.	precommunicative
7. We can also tell that this child understands how to form _____ and that writing progresses from left to right.	letters
8. This child has probably not yet acquired an understanding of the _____ principle.	alphabetic

Look at this writing from a six-year-old child: Me ND Jese DEAGO r fnz (Me and Jesse Diego are friends.)	
9. This child is probably in the _____ phase of developmental spelling because most sounds are represented phonetically.	phonetic
10. We can also tell that this child has developed a good sense of phonemic _____.	awareness
11. This child probably believes that words are typically spelled the way that they _____. Soon, this child will learn that not all words are spelled this way.	sound

Look at this writing from another six-year-old child:
 	
    I luv my Tarus that was a car adn I luv my mom adn my dad adn we wtch TV.
    (I love my Taurus, that was a car, and I love my mom and dad, and we watch TV.)	

12. This child is probably in the _____ phase. Many words are spelled correctly, although the sight word *and* is regularly misspelled. Several words are still being spelled the way this child _____ them rather than as sight words.	transitional hears
13. We can tell, however, that this child is beyond the phonetic phase and no longer believes that each word is _____ as it sounds.	spelled
14. This child's understanding of phonemic awareness is fairly well developed because most _____ are represented in writing.	sounds

PRACTICAL EXAMPLES AND RESOURCES FOR UNDERSTANDING DEVELOPMENTAL SPELLING PATTERNS IN YOUR CLASSROOM

Take a Look Videos

Take a look at this video of a primary grade teacher: http://bit.ly/1LFiMV9.

A first grade teacher demonstrates how to use an understanding of developmental, or invented, spelling to help her students with classroom writing activities.

Take a look at this video of a young child: http://bit.ly/1F0jCHm.

This young child, in an early stage of developmental spelling, tries to read a story she wrote to her mother.

Lesson Suggestions

Teaching Short-Vowel Discrimination Using Dr. Seuss Rhymes (http://bit.ly/1DxpmaN).

An activity that shows students short vowel word families, which is an important transition in developmental spelling.

Spelling Patterns: "Go Fish" Card Game (http://bit.ly/1HNBMkV).

Students make a set of cards and then play "Go Fish," a card game designed to help them learn several common English spelling patterns.

Sort, Hunt, Write: A Weekly Spelling Program (http://bit.ly/16nmdQx).

A preassessment determines each student's developmental stage. Then students create individual word lists to learn spelling patterns most appropriate for each student individually, with partners, and in small groups.

Apps for Classroom Use

Spelling 1-2: http://bit.ly/1KIVGK4

Current cost: $4.99

Allows students to work on their own words to become a super speller. Includes personal spelling lists as well as over 2,000 first and second grade level words.

Montessori Crosswords: http://bit.ly/1zT2hi8

Current cost: $2.99

Students develop reading and writing skills by playing with words and hearing letters and words sounded out in a fun, playful fashion.

 ## Online Reading Resources

To learn more about developmental spelling patterns, explore these online resources:

- Lutz, E. (1986). Invented spelling and spelling development. (An online article that describes the stages in spelling development and the implications of this understanding for instruction.)

  Retrieved from http://www.readingrockets.org/article/267

  Manning, M. (2004). Invented spelling. *Teaching K–8.* (Online Journal.) (Describes how young writers make the transition from "inventive" to "conventional" spellers.)

  Retrieved from http://bit.ly/1zvHHEg

- Jones, L. (2005). *The do's and don'ts of invented spelling.* (A short article describing what to do in the classroom and what not to do, with respect to invented, or developmental, spelling.)

  Retrieved from http://edcate.co/1tXuGnH

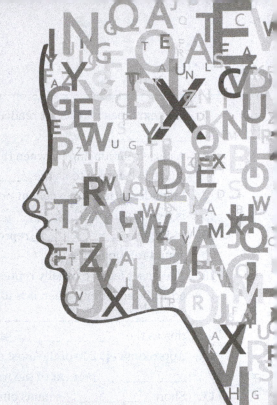

Posttest I

Take this posttest and then compare your answers with the answers provided on pages 122–124.

1. On a separate sheet of paper, define the following central terms that are important in understanding word analysis principles:
   - *phoneme*
   - *grapheme*
   - *phonemic awareness*
   - *phonological awareness*
   - *onset patterns*
   - *rime patterns*
   - *consonant digraph*
   - *consonant blend*
   - *context clues*
   - *sight words*
   - *phonetic phase*
   - *semiphonetic phase*
   - *precommunicative phase*
   - *morpheme*
   - *affix*
   - *closed syllables*
   - *open syllables*
   - *pronunciation entry*

2. Readers use word _____ strategies to analyze written words to construct word sounds and meanings.

3. The spoken word *mast* has _____ phonemes.

4. The spoken word *ship* has _____ phonemes.

5. Context clues may assist readers with both _____ and
    _____.

6. A close relationship between the letters and sounds in a language is referred to as the _____ principle.

7. In kindergarten, an excellent predictor of later reading success is a child's level of _____ awareness.

8. In English, _____ represent the most consistent letter–sound relationships.

9. The onset letter <u>c</u> usually represents the sound associated with the letter <u>s</u> when it is followed by the vowel letters _____, _____, or _____. We refer to this as the "_____ <u>c</u>" sound.

10. Approximately 200 of the most common words account for about _____ percent of the words in most reading selections.

11. Short _____ sounds often appear in a syllable or single-syllable word that ends in a consonant or consonant cluster.

12. _____ vowels are neither long nor short. They have a sound determined by the _____ r.

13. <u>Y</u> represents a vowel sound when it appears at the _____ of a word.

14. A digraph represents _____ sound. A _____ represents a blending of two vowel sounds.

15. A _____ vowel sound is usually produced when two vowels appear side by side.

16. Words that are recognized and pronounced automatically are called _____ words.

17. Match the vowel sound represented by the underlined letter(s) in the words in Column A with the type of vowel sound in Column B by placing the number of the type of vowel sound in Column B in the space in front of the word in Column A.

A	B
_____ <u>e</u>gg	1. long (glided)
_____ g<u>o</u>	2. short (unglided)
_____ s<u>i</u>de	3. r-controlled
_____ j<u>oy</u>	4. diphthong
_____ c<u>ow</u>	
_____ c<u>or</u>d	
_____ ch<u>ea</u>p	
_____ beg<u>i</u>n	
_____ p<u>ou</u>t	
_____ l<u>a</u>p	

18. Place an <u>L</u> in the space in front of the word in Column A if the underlined vowel represents a long sound and an <u>S</u> if it represents a short sound. Then select the reason for the vowel sound in Column B and place the appropriate number in the space after the word in Column A. The first one is done for you.

A	B
<u>L</u> beg<u>i</u>n <u>3</u>	1. final <u>e</u>
____ p<u>e</u>ncil _____	2. vowel digraph
____ p<u>ai</u>n _____	3. open syllable
____ r<u>o</u>pe _____	4. closed syllable
____ pr<u>ea</u>cher _____	
____ d<u>i</u>graph _____	
____ s<u>i</u>mple _____	
____ f<u>a</u>te _____	

19. Match the principle for syllabication in Column B with the word in Column A by placing the number of the visual clue in the space in front of the word in Column A.

A	B
_____ turtle	1. V/CV
_____ unclear	2. VC/CV
_____ airtight	3. VC/(blend) V
_____ overt	4. VR/V
_____ oral	5. /C-le
_____ mental	6. compound word
_____ simple	7. prefix
_____ belongs	
_____ preview	
_____ football	
_____ peril	
_____ hundred	

20. If a dictionary entry appeared as follows:

refuse (*n.*)

ref·use   \'re-ˌfyüs, -ˌfyüz\

(a) what is its part of speech? _____

(b) which syllable is stressed? _____

(c) Would the word's pronunciation fit into the following sentence? *I refuse to pay that bill!* _____

1. Definitions

phoneme	The smallest single unit of sound in a language that distinguishes one *morpheme* (meaning unit) from another. (See chapters 1 and 2.)
grapheme	A written or printed representation of a phoneme. (See chapter 1.)
phonemic awareness	The awareness of individual sounds or phonemes as objects that can be analyzed and manipulated. (See chapters 1 and 2.)
phonological awareness	The awareness of individual words and syllables as objects that can be analyzed and manipulated. (See chapters 1 and 2.)
onset patterns	Initial consonant letters found at the *beginning* of syllables and words, such as b, c, d, f, g, sn, st, or str. (See chapter 3.)
rime patterns	A limited set of the most common *endings* to syllables and words, such as -ake, -ack, -ail, or -ame. (See chapter 3.)
consonant digraph	Two different consonant letters that appear together and represent a single sound, or phoneme, that is not usually associated with either letter. (See chapter 3.)
consonant blend	Two or three consecutive consonant letters, each representing a separate phoneme that are blended together. (See chapter 3.)
context clues	Information around a word that provides assistance in determining its pronunciation and meaning. (See chapter 5.)
sight words	Words recognized automatically without conscious attention. (See chapter 6.)
phonetic phase	A phase in developmental spelling where writing looks like a child is trying to represent nearly every sound in each word by spelling it as it sounds. (See chapter 10.)
semiphonetic phase	A phase in developmental spelling where children use writing to communicate meaning, but words are often represented only by the initial letter sound. More consonants than vowels appear. (See chapter 10.)
precommunicative phase	A phase in developmental spelling where writing is characterized by not having a consistent communicative intent. (See chapter 10.)
morpheme	The smallest unit of meaning in a language. (See chapter 7.)
affix	A prefix or a suffix. (See chapter 7.)
closed syllables	A syllable ending with a consonant letter, which usually makes the vowel sound short. (See chapter 8.)
open syllables	A syllable ending with a vowel letter, which usually makes the vowel sound long. (See chapter 8.)
pronunciation	The entry in a dictionary that provides information about a word's pronunciation. (See chapter 9.)

2. analysis (See chapter 1.)

3. four (See chapter 2.)

4. three (See chapter 2.)

5. pronunciation, meaning (See chapter 5.)

6. alphabetic (See chapter 2.)

7. phonemic (See chapter 7.)

8. consonants (See chapter 3.)

9. e, i, y, soft (See chapter 3.)

10. 50 (See chapter 6.)

11. vowel (See chapter 4.)

12. R-controlled, following (See chapter 4.)

13. end (See chapter 4.)

14. one, blend (diphthong) (See chapter 4.)

15. long (See chapter 4.)

16. sight (See chapter 6.)

17. Matching vowels (See chapter 4.)

    2 egg   (short or unglided)

    1 go   (long or glided)

    1 side   (long or glided)

    4 joy   (diphthong)

    4 cow   (diphthong)

    3 cord   (r-controlled)

    1 cheap   (long or glided)

    2 begin   (short or unglided)

    4 pout   (diphthong)

    2 lap   (short or unglided)

18. Long and short vowels (chapter 4.)

    L begin   3

    S pencil   4

    L pain   2

    L rope   1

    L preacher   2

    L digraph   3

    S simple   4

    L fate   1

19. Syllabication (See chapter 8.)

    5 turtle

    7 unclear

    6 airtight

    1 overt

    4 oral

    2 mental

5 simple

1 belongs

7 preview

6 football

4 peril

3 hundred

20. (a) noun   (See chapter 9.)

    (b) first   (See chapter 9.)

    (c) no [It would fit into a sentence such as, *"Put your refuse into the trash bin, to be taken out with the garbage."*]

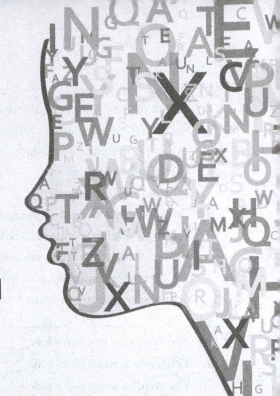

Posttest II

Take this posttest and then compare your answers with the answers provided on pages 128–130.

1. On a separate sheet of paper, define the following central terms that are important to understanding word analysis principles:
   - *diphthong*
   - *graphophonic*
   - *phonemic awareness*
   - *prefix*
   - *VCV pattern*
   - *vowel*
   - *grapheme*
   - *inflectional ending*
   - *morpheme*
   - *phonics*
   - *orthography*
   - *consonant cluster*
   - r-controlled vowel
   - *semiphonetic phase*
   - *alphabetic principle*
   - *word analysis strategies*
   - *guide words*
   - *closed syllable*

2. Which of the following is the best predictor of later reading success for kindergarten children? _____
   (a) graphophonic knowledge
   (b) phonemic awareness
   (c) syllabication knowledge

3. True or false: Context clues assist readers in predicting and con-firming meaning, but pronunciation is accessed through word analysis clues other than context. _____

4. What are the four types of clues authors provide that read-ers can use as context clues? _____, _____, _____, and _____

5. The spoken word *poles* has _____ morphemes.

6. The spoken word *poles* has _____ phonemes.

7. The written word *poles* has _____ graphemes.

8. The written word *poles* has _____ alphabetic letters.

9. Approximately 400 of the most common words account for about _____ percent of the words in most reading selections.

10. A digraph represents _____ sound. A _____ represents a blending of two vowel sounds.

11. High-frequency words are usually also _____ _____ for most readers.

12. Match the vowel sound represented by the underlined letter(s) in the words in Column A with the type of vowel sound in Column B by placing the number of the type of vowel sound in Column B in the space in front of the word in Column A.

A	B
_____ <u>a</u>m	1. long (glided)
_____ m<u>e</u>	2. short (unglided)
_____ pr<u>i</u>de	3. <u>r</u>-controlled
_____ t<u>oy</u>	4. diphthong
_____ gl<u>ow</u>	
_____ b<u>ir</u>d	
_____ b<u>ea</u>t	
_____ sl<u>i</u>m	
_____ p<u>ou</u>t	
_____ l<u>a</u>p	

13. Place an <u>L</u> in the space in front of the word in Column A if the underlined vowel represents the long sound and an <u>S</u> if it represents a short sound. Then select the reason for the vowel sound in Column B and place the appropriate number in the space behind the word in Column A. The first one is done for you.

A		B
__L__ t<u>o</u>ken ____3____		1. final <u>e</u>
_____ l<u>e</u>ntil _____		2. vowel digraph
_____ r<u>ai</u>n _____		3. open syllable
_____ sl<u>o</u>pe _____		4. closed syllable
_____ t<u>ea</u>cher _____		
_____ d<u>i</u>graph _____		
_____ d<u>i</u>mple _____		
_____ g<u>a</u>te _____		

14. Match the principle for syllabication in Column B with the word in Column A by placing the number of the visual clue in the space in front of the word in Column A.

A	B
_____ castle	1. V/CV
_____ undo	2. VC/CV
_____ staircase	3. VC/(blend) V
_____ open	4. VR/V
_____ army	5. C-le
_____ magma	6. compound word
_____ dimple	7. prefix
_____ cement	
_____ return	
_____ doorway	
_____ urban	
_____ hundred	

15. Consider the following two dictionary entries:

    (a) lead (*n.*) \lēd\

    (b) lead (*n.*) \lĕd\

    Which pronunciation, (a) or (b), would be used in the following sentences:

    (c) *She is the lead in a hit television show.* _____

    (d) *Lead is an important metal that has many uses.*

    _____

16. Being able to identify the initial consonant sound in a word such as *sit* is an example of _____ awareness.

17. Being able to clap each syllable in a word is an example of _____.
    (a) phonemic awareness
    (b) phonological awareness
    (c) syllabication awareness

18. The onset letter <u>c</u> usually represents the sound associated with the letter <u>k</u> when it is followed by the vowel letters _____, _____, or _____.

19. True or false: When dividing compound words into syllables, each word is usually its own syllable. _____

20. If a word ends in <u>le</u>, explain the process you would use to decide on that word's last syllable.

ANSWERS TO POSTTEST II

1. Definitions

diphthong	A type of vowel cluster that is sometimes called a vowel blend, where two vowel letters appear together and represent a blending of the sounds associated with each letter. (See chapter 4.)
graphophonic	The relationship between sounds in our language and the written letters or spelling patterns. (See chapter 1.)
phonemic awareness	The awareness of individual sounds or phonemes as objects that can be analyzed and manipulated. (See chapters 1 and 2.)
prefix	An affix added to the beginning of root words to change their meanings. (See chapter 7.)
VCV pattern	A vowel-consonant-vowel pattern. A generalization for syllabication that suggests the division appears after the first vowel in the pattern. (See chapter 8.)
vowel	Sounds produced without a restriction in the airstream, represented by the five letters <u>a</u>, <u>e</u>, <u>i</u>, <u>o</u>, <u>u</u>, and sometimes <u>y</u> and <u>w</u>. (See chapter 4.)
grapheme	A written or printed representation of a phoneme. (See chapter 1.)
inflectional ending	An affix added to the end of a root word; it often changes the grammatical function but not the core meaning of the root word to which it is added. (See chapter 7.)
morpheme	The smallest unit of meaning in a language. (See chapters 1 and 7.)
phonics	The application of information about the sounds of language to the teaching of reading and the knowledge about how sounds are represented by letters or letter combinations in written language to help readers determine the oral equivalents of unfamiliar words. (See chapter 1.)

orthography	The writing system of a language. (See chapter 1.)
consonant cluster	Consonant clusters include two or three consonant letters that often appear together. There are two types: digraphs and blends. (See chapter 3.)
r-controlled vowel	Vowels that are neither long nor short but have a sound determined largely by the following r. (See chapters 4 and 8.)
semiphonetic phase	A phase in developmental spelling where children use writing to communicate meaning, but words are often represented only by the initial letter sound. More consonants than vowels appear. (See chapter 10.)
alphabetic principle	The close relationship between the letters and sounds in a language. (See chapters 2 and 3.)
word analysis strategies	Strategies that permit you to determine both the sounds of words and their meanings. Word analysis strategies include phonological and phonemic awareness, phonics, context use, sight word knowledge, morphemic and structural analysis, and dictionary skills. (See chapter 1.)
guide words	Words that appear at the top of each page in the body of a dictionary to help readers locate particular words quickly. (See chapter 9.)
closed syllable	A syllable ending with a consonant letter, usually making the vowel sound short. (See chapter 8.)

2. (b) phonemic awareness (See chapters 1 and 2.)

3. False (See chapter 5.)

4. definition, synonym, example, mood (See chapter 5.)

5. two (See chapters 1 and 8.)

6. four (See chapters 1 and 2.)

7. four (See chapters 1 and 8.)

8. five (See chapter 1.)

9. 70 (See chapter 6.)

10. one (See chapter 4.)

    blend (diphthong) (See chapter 4.)

11. sight words (See chapter 6.)

12. Matching vowels (See chapter 4.)

    2 am

    1 me

    1 pride

    4 toy

    1 glow

    3 bird

    1 beat

    2 slim

    4 pout

    2 lap

13. Long and short vowels (See chapter 4.)

L t<u>o</u>ken   3

S l<u>e</u>ntil   4

L r<u>ai</u>n   2

L sl<u>o</u>pe   1

L t<u>ea</u>cher   2

L d<u>i</u>graph   3

S d<u>i</u>mple   4

L g<u>a</u>te   1

14. Syllabication (See chapter 8.)

5 castle

7 undo

6 staircase

1 open

4 army

2 magma

5 dimple

1 cement

7 return

6 doorway

2 urban

3 hundred

15. (c) a (See chapter 9.)

(d) b (See chapter 9.)

16. phonemic (See chapter 2.)

17. (b) phonological awareness (See chapter 2.)

18. <u>o</u>, <u>a</u>, <u>u</u> (See chapter 3.)

19. True (See chapter 8.)

20. If the letter before the <u>le</u> is a consonant, the consonant plus <u>le</u> form the last syllable. (See chapter 8.)

References

Included in this section are references that:

1. contain suggestions for teaching word analysis strategies to children;
2. provide additional information about English orthography;
3. examine issues related to word analysis; or
4. report research related to word analysis and spelling.

Some older references are included because they are classic works that still inform the field.

Acker, B. C. (2009). *Using context clues: A third grade lesson by Mrs. Acker*. Retrieved from http://www.authorstream.com/Presentation/grrrlish-200334-using-context-clues-education-ppt-powerpoint/

Adams, M. J. (1990). *Beginning to read: Thinking and learning about print*. Cambridge, MA: MIT Press.

Adams, M. J., Foorman, B. R., Lundberg, I., & Beeler, T. (1998). *Phonemic awareness in young children*. Baltimore, MD: Paul H. Brookes.

Anonymous. (2004). *Tips for teachers: Syllabication rules*. Phoenix, AZ: Reading Manipulatives. Retrieved from http://www.readskill.com/media/pdf/syllabication7.pdf

Anonymous. (2007). Reading lesson: Vowel sounds. *YouTube*. Retrieved from http://www.youtube.com/watch?v=ml6xYqYLb3E&feature=related

Anonymous. (2010). *Phonological and phonemic awareness*. Reading Rockets. Washington, DC: WETA. Retrieved from http://www.readingrockets.org/helping/target/phonologicalphonemic

Anonymous. (2010). Reading lesson: Introduce onset-rime blending. *YouTube*. Retrieved from http://www.youtube.com/watch?v=MEEc5Pt5WV8

Anonymous. (n.d.). Morphemic analysis. *YouTube*. Retrieved from http://www.youtube.com/watch?v=WM2tC16nrBgApel, K. (2014). A comprehensive definition of morphological awareness: Implications for assessment. *Topics in Language Disorders, 34*(3), 197–209.

Ball, E. W., & Blachman, B. A. (1991). Does phoneme awareness training in kindergarten make a difference in early word recognition and developmental spelling? *Reading Research Quarterly, 26*, 49–66.

Baumann, J. F., Edwards, E. C., Font, G., Tereshinski, C. A., Kame'enui, E. J., & Olejnik, S. (2002). Teaching morphemic and contextual analysis to fifth-grade students. *Reading Research Quarterly, 37*, 150–176. Retrieved from http://128.220.219.39/olms/data/resource/2041/la_vocab_research.pdf

Baumann, J. F., Hoffman, J. V., Moon, J., & Duffy-Hester, A. M. (1998). Where are teachers' voices in the phonics/whole language debate? Results from a survey of U.S. elementary classroom teachers. *The Reading Teacher, 51*, 636–650.

Bear, D. R. (Ed.). (1999). *Words their way: Word study for phonics, vocabulary, and spelling instruction* (2nd ed.). Upper Saddle River, NJ: Prentice Hall.

Bear, D. R., & Templeton, S. (1998). Explorations in developmental spelling: Foundations for learning and teaching phonics, spelling, and vocabulary. *The Reading Teacher, 52*, 222–242.

Blachman, B. A. (1994). What we have learned from longitudinal studies of phonological processing and reading, and some unanswered questions: A response to Torgesen, Wagner, and Rashotte. *Journal of Learning Disabilities, 27*, 287–291.

Brummitt-Yale, J. (2010). Phonemic awareness vs. phonological awareness. *K-12 Reader*. Retrieved from http://www.k12reader.com/phonemic-awareness-vs-phonological-awareness/

Bryant, P., Nunes, T., & Barros, R. (2014). The connection between children's knowledge and use of grapho-phonic and morphemic units in written text and their learning at school. *British Journal of Educational Psychology, 84*(2), 211–225.

Canney, G., & Schreiner, R. (1976–1977). A study of the effectiveness of selected syllabication rules and phonogram patterns for word attack. *Reading Research Quarterly, 12*, 102–124.

Case, A. (2008). Why does my teacher make me use an English-English dictionary? *UsingEnglish.com*. Retrieved from http://www.usingenglish.com/articles/why-does-my-teacher-make-me-use-an-englishenglish-dictionary.html

Chomsky, C. (1970). Reading, writing, and phonology. *Harvard Educational Review, 40*, 287–309.

Clay, M. M. (1991). *Becoming literate: The construction of inner control*. Portsmouth, NH: Heinemann Educational Books.

Clymer, T. (1963). The utility of phonics generalizations in the primary grades. *The Reading Teacher, 16*, 252–258.

Cunningham, P. M. (2000). *Phonics they use: Words for reading and writing* (3rd ed.). New York: Longman.

Cunningham, P. M., & Cunningham, J. W. (1992). Making words: Enhancing the invented spelling-decoding connection. *The Reading Teacher*, 106–115.

Cunningham, P. M., & Cunningham, J. W. (2000). What we know about how to teach phonics. In S. E. Farstrup & S. J. Samuels (Eds.), *What research has to say about reading instruction* (pp. 87–109). Newark, DE: International Reading Association. Retrieved from: http://www.learner.org/workshops/readingk2/support/How ToTeachPhonics_1.pdf http://www.learner.org/workshops/readingk2/support/How ToTeachPhonics_2.pdf http://www.learner.org/workshops/readingk2/support/How ToTeachPhonics_3.pdf

Davidson, J. L. (Ed.). (1988). *Counterpoint and beyond: A response to becoming a nation of readers*. Urbana, IL: National Council of Teachers of English.

Duffelmeyer, F. A., & Black, J. L. (1996). The names test: A domain-specific validation study. *The Reading Teacher, 50*, 148–150.

Duffelmeyer, F. A., Kruse, A. E., Merkley, D. J., & Fyfe, S. A. (1994). Further validation and enhancement of the names test. *The Reading Teacher, 48*, 118–128.

Durkin, D. (1974). Phonics: Instruction that needs to be improved. *The Reading Teacher, 28*, 152–157.

Durkin, D. (1981). *Strategies for identifying words*. Boston, MA: Allyn & Bacon.

Ehri, L. C. (2014). Orthographic mapping in the acquisition of sight word reading, spelling memory, and vocabulary learning. *Scientific Studies of Reading, 18*(1), 5–21.

Ehri, L. C., Nunes, S., Willows, D., Schuster, B., Yaghoub-Zadeh, Z., & Shanahan, T. (2001). Phonemic awareness instruction helps children learn to read: Evidence from the National Reading Panel's meta-analysis. *Reading Research Quarterly, 36*(3), 250–287.

Ericson, L., & Juliebo, M. F. (1998). *The phonological awareness handbook for kindergarten and primary teachers*. Newark, DE: International Reading Association.

Fisher, D., & Frey, N. (2014). Scaffolded reading instruction of content area texts. *The Reading Teacher, 67*(5), 347–351.

Foorman, B., & Torgesen, J. D. (2001). Critical elements of classroom and small group instruction to promote reading success in all children. *Learning Disabilities Research and Practice, 16*, 103–121.

Fraser, C. A. (1999). The role of consulting a dictionary in reading and vocabulary learning. *Canadian Journal of Applied Linguistics. 2*, 73–89.

Freppon, P. A., & Dahl, K. L. (1991). Learning about phonics in a whole language classroom. *Language Arts, 68*, 190–197.

Fries-Gaither, J. (2008). Teacher resources for making inferences, using context clues. *Beyond penguins and polar bears: An online magazine for K-5 teachers*. (2). Retrieved from http://beyondpenguins.nsdl.org/issue/column.php?date=April2008&departmentid=professional&columnid=professional!literacy

Fry, E. (2004). *1000 Instant words: The most common words for teaching reading, writing and spelling*. Westminster, CA: Teacher Created Resources.

Fry, E. B., & Kress, J. B. (2006). *The reading teacher's book of lists* (5th ed.). Indianapolis, IN: Jossey-Bass.

Gaskins, I. W. (2004). Word detectives. *Educational Leadership: What Research Says about Reading, 61*(6), 70–73.

Gillet, J. W., & Temple, C. (1994). *Understanding reading problems: Assessment and instruction* (4th ed.). Glenview, IL: Scott Foresman.

Groff, P. (1998). Where's the phonics? Making a case for its direct and systematic instruction. *The Reading Teacher, 52*, 138–142.

Gunning, T. G. (1995). Word building: A strategic approach to the teaching of phonics. *The Reading Teacher, 48*, 484–488.

Hiebert, E. H., Brown, Z. A., Taitague, C., Fisher, C. W., & Adler, M. A. (2004). Texts and English language learners: Scaffolding entrée to reading. In F. B. Boyd, C. H. Brock, & M. S. Rozendal (Eds.), *Multicultural and multilingual literacy and language: Contexts and practices* (pp. 32–53). New York: Guilford Press.

Hull, M. A. (1998). *Phonics for the teacher of reading* (7th ed.). Upper Saddle River, NJ: Merrill/Prentice Hall.

International Literacy Association. (1997). *The role of phonics in reading instruction: A position statement from the Board of Directors of the International Literacy Association.* Newark, DE: International Literacy Association.

International Literacy Association. (1998). *Phonemic awareness and the teaching of reading: A position statement from the Board of Directors of the International Literacy Association.* Newark, DE: International Literacy Association.

Johnston, R., McGeown, S., & Moxon, G. E. (2014). Towards an understanding of how children read and spell irregular words: The role of nonword and orthographic processing skills. *Journal of Research in Reading, 37*(1), 51–64.

Johnston, R. S., & Watson, J. E. (2004). Accelerating the development of reading, spelling and phonemic awareness skills in initial readers. *Reading and Writing, 17*, 327–357.

Jones, L. (2005). *The do's and don'ts of invented spelling.* Retrieved from http://www.education.com/magazine/article/The_Dos_and_Donts_Invented/

Juel, C. (1991). Beginning reading. In R. Barr, M. L. Kamil, P. B. Mosenthat, & P. D. Pearson (Eds.), *Handbook of reading research* (2nd ed., pp. 759–788). New York: Longman.

Juel, C., & Deffes, R. (2004). Making words stick. *Educational Leadership: What Research Says about Reading, 61*(6), 30–34.

Knight-McKenna, M. (2008). Syllable types: A strategy for reading multisyllabic words. *Teaching Exceptional Children.* Retrieved from http://findarticles.com/p/articles/mi_7749/is_200801/ai_n32259536/

Lapp, D., & Flood, J. (1997). Where's the phonics? Making the case (again) for integrated code instruction. *The Reading Teacher, 50*, 696–700.

Larabee, K. M., Burns, M. K., & McComas, J. J. (2014). Effects of an iPad-supported phonics intervention on decoding performance and time on-task. *Journal of Behavioral Education, 23*(4), 449–469.

Leu, D. J., Jr., & Kinzer, C. K. (2003). *Effective literacy instruction, K–8: Implementing best practice* (5th ed.). Upper Saddle River, NJ: Prentice Hall.

Lewis, L. (2008). All about words: Dictionary activities. *Education World.* Available at: http://www.educationworld.com/a_lesson/lesson/lesson206.shtml

Lyon, G. R., & Chhabra, V. (2004). The science of reading research. *Educational Leadership: What Research Says about Reading, 61*(6), 13–17.

Manning, M. (2004). Invented spelling. *Teaching pre-k-8.* Retrieved from http://www.teachingk-8.com/archives/celebrations_in_reading_and_writing/invented_spelling_by_maryann_manning.html

McGeown, S. P., & Medford, E. (2014). Using method of instruction to predict the skills supporting initial reading development: Insight from a synthetic phonics approach. *Reading and Writing, 27*(3), 591–608.

Morrow, L. M. (1993). *Literacy development in the early years* (2nd ed.). Boston, MA: Allyn & Bacon.

Morrow, L. M., & Tracey, D. H. (1997). Strategies used for phonics instruction in early childhood classrooms. *The Reading Teacher, 50*, 644–651.

Mountain, L. (2005). ROOTing out meaning: More morphemic analysis for primary pupils. *The Reading Teacher, 58*, 742–749. Retrieved from http://www.reading.org/Publish.aspx?pageRT-58-8-Mountain.pdf&moderetrieve&D10.1598/RT.58.8.4&FRT-58-8-Mountain.pdf&key225E3AF4-9689-46FB-8A67-1B760EC68B5C

National Reading Panel. (2000). *Report of the National Reading Panel.* Washington, DC: U.S. Government.

Owens, K. (2009). *Phonics on the web.* An online tutorial exploring many aspects of phonics. Retrieved from http://www.phonicson-theweb.com/index.php

Pacheco, M. B., & Goodwin, A. P. (2013). Putting two and two together: Middle school students' morphological problem solving strategies for unknown words. *Journal of Adolescent & Adult Literacy, 56*(7), 541–553.

Parault Dowds, S. J., Haverback, H. R., & Parkinson, M. M. (2014). Classifying the context clues in children's text. *The Journal of Experimental Education,* (ahead-of-print), 1–22.

Parlapiano, E. (2010). Sounding out phonics. *Parents.* Retrieved from http://www2.scholastic.com/browse/article.jsp?id=10219

Perfetti, C. A., Beck, I., Bell, L., & Hughes, C. (1987). Phonemic knowledge and learning to read are reciprocal: A longitudinal study of first grade children. *Merrill-Palmer Quarterly, 33*, 283–319.

Powell, D., & Hornsby, D. (1993). *Learning phonics and spelling in a whole language classroom.* New York: Scholastic Professional Books.

Reiner, K. (1998). Developing a kindergarten phonemic awareness program: An action research project. *The Reading Teacher, 52*, 70–73.

Shanker, J. (2007). *Developing phonics knowledge: Vowels.* Upper Saddle River, NJ: Allyn & Bacon. Available at: http://www.education.com/reference/article/developing-phonics-knowledge-vowels/

Smith, F. (1994). *Understanding reading* (5th ed.). Hillsdale, NJ: Lawrence Erlbaum Associates.

Snow, C. M., Burns, S., & Griffin, P. (Eds.). (1998). *Preventing reading difficulties in young children.* Washington, DC: National Academy Press.

Stahl, S. A. (1992). Saying the "p" word: Nine guidelines for exemplary phonics instruction. *The Reading Teacher, 45*, 618–625.

Stanovich, K. E. (1994). Romance and reality. *The Reading Teacher, 47*, 280–291.

Staudt, D. (2009). Intensive word study and repeated reading improves reading skills for two students with learning disabilities. *The Reading Teacher, 63*(2), 142–151. Retrieved from http://www.reading.org/Publish.aspx?page=RT-63-2-Staudt.pdf&mode=retrieve&D=10.1598/RT.63.2.5&F=RT-63-2-Staudt.pdf&key=97A82610-E13D-404A-9978-E8AF56654E95

Strickland, D. S. (1995). Reinventing our literacy programs: Books, basics, balance. *The Reading Teacher, 48*, 294–302.

Strickland, D. S. (1998). *Teaching phonics today: A primer for educators.* Newark, NJ: International Reading Association.

Suggate, S. P. (2014). A meta-analysis of the long-term effects of phonemic awareness, phonics, fluency, and reading comprehension interventions. *Journal of Learning Disabilities.* Retrieved from http://ldx.sagepub.com/content/early/2014/04/04/0022219414528540.

U.S. Department of Education. Center for the Improvement of Early Reading Achievement. (2001). *Put reading first: The research building blocks for teaching children to read.* Washington, DC: GPO.

Weaver, C. (1990). *Understanding whole language: From principles to practice.* Portsmouth, NH: Heinemann Educational Books.

Yopp, H. K. (1992). Developing phonemic awareness in young children. *The Reading Teacher, 45*, 696–703.